CW01391338

The National Archives History Toolkit for Primary Schools

Clare Horrie and Rachel Hillman

BLOOMSBURY EDUCATION

LONDON OXFORD NEW YORK NEW DELHI SYDNEY

BLOOMSBURY EDUCATION
Bloomsbury Publishing Plc
50 Bedford Square, London, WC1B 3DP, UK

BLOOMSBURY, BLOOMSBURY EDUCATION and the Diana logo are trademarks of
Bloomsbury Publishing Plc

The National Archives logo device is a trademark of The National Archives and is used under licence

First published in Great Britain, 2020

Text copyright © Clare Horrie and Rachel Hillman, 2020

Images Crown Copyright © Reproduced with permission of The National Archives, 2020
(unless otherwise stated)

The National Archives logo © Crown Copyright, 2020

Clare Horrie and Rachel Hillman have asserted their rights under the Copyright,
Designs and Patents Act, 1988, to be identified as Authors of this work

Every reasonable effort has been made to trace copyright holders of material reproduced in this book,
but if any have been inadvertently overlooked the publishers would be glad to hear from them

Bloomsbury Publishing Plc does not have any control over, or responsibility for, any third-party
websites referred to or in this book. All internet addresses given in this book were correct at the time of
going to press. The author and publisher regret any inconvenience caused if addresses have changed or
sites have ceased to exist, but can accept no responsibility for any such changes

All rights reserved. This book may be photocopied for use in the educational establishment for which
it was purchased, but may not be reproduced in any other form or by any other means – graphic,
electronic, or mechanical, including photocopying, recording, taping or information storage or retrieval
systems – without prior permission in writing from the publishers

A catalogue record for this book is available from the British Library

ISBN: PB: 978-1-4729-5935-5; ePDF: 978-1-4729-5936-2; ePub: 978-1-4729-5934-8

2 4 6 8 10 9 7 5 3 1 (paperback)

Text design by Marcus Duck Design

Printed and bound in the UK by CPI Group (UK) Ltd., Croydon, CR0 4YY

MIX
Paper from
responsible sources
FSC
www.fsc.org   FSC® C013604

All papers used by Bloomsbury Publishing Plc are natural, recyclable products from wood grown in
well managed forests. The manufacturing processes conform to the environmental regulations of the
country of origin

To find out more about our authors and books visit www.bloomsbury.com and sign up for
our newsletters

Contents

Introduction

This book contains a series of lessons that we hope will transform your pupils' learning experience in history by introducing them to the concept that different sources can be used as evidence to investigate and understand the past. All lessons support the delivery of the Key Stage 1 and Key Stage 2 National Curriculum for history and relate to a particular topic, theme or requirement in the curriculum. Our core purpose is to support the central premise of the curriculum that all pupils should understand the importance of historical enquiry. Each lesson is based on a single enquiry question approached through a starter activity, a main activity and a creative activity. The lessons can be used or adapted for teaching particular topics and incorporated into a general scheme of work.

Working with sources in the primary classroom

The range of sources for teachers to use within the primary school history classroom is immense. The following sources form the basis of the lessons outlined in this book: photographs, census data, government reports, cartoons, diagrams, posters, police reports, trial documents, seals, manuscripts, maps, and private and official letters. We hope that encounter with such a rich range of source types will expose pupils to the stuff of history and strengthen their skills in handling primary evidence, forming their own interpretations and the ability to read between the lines. The sources selected mainly come from The National Archives collection and are not readily found in existing textbooks. They offer a unique way for primary school pupils to access real historical documents rather than work with word-processed extracts or illustrations published in textbooks.

All of the sources included in this book support National Curriculum content guidelines. Teachers looking for sources relating to such content themes as changes within living memory of national importance, events beyond living memory, the lives of significant individuals, and significant historical events, people and places in their locality will find relevant lessons in this book. High-resolution versions of sources are provided online at www.bloomsbury.com/primary-history-toolkit so you can display them on an interactive whiteboard, print copies out for use in the classroom or integrate them into your teaching tools. Where required, transcripts and simplified transcripts of written sources are provided in the book and can be photocopied and handed out to pupils.

All lessons can be adapted to your particular classroom, the pupils you are teaching and how you deliver your particular scheme of work. You may prefer to split the activities over two or more lessons accordingly.

The 'mystery document' approach

The 'mystery document' activity provides an exciting way to use sources to get children interested in a new history topic. It involves them in active learning from the very beginning of the lesson, encouraging them to make their own observations and to ask their own questions. Children become the detectives, trying to piece together what a document or image can reveal, sparking their interest and their desire to find out more about the topic. You can use this approach with any of the sources in the book and it makes a great starter activity for any history lesson. We refer to the approach throughout the book, so here are some general tips on leading the activity and getting it right.

Print out copies of the source or display a large version of it on a whiteboard. Don't say anything about the source at this point. Give the pupils five to ten minutes to look closely at the source and to start making their own observations. You could use the following prompts:

- Look at the document as an object. If there is any text, DON'T read it. What do you see?

- How was it produced? For example, was it typed, handwritten, drawn or painted?

- If it is a written document, how is the text set out on the page? For example, are there any dates or short sentences?

- What does this reveal about the type of document it could be? For example, dates may indicate a diary or a letter, and short sentences may indicate a report.

- When was it written? Can you see a date?

- Are there any other points to note?

After the pupils have had a go at making some observations, encourage them to read or describe what they see in the source and to make inferences based on its contents. If you're looking at a written document, ask them now to READ it. What else can we tell about it from the contents? The following questions may be useful:

- Can we tell when it was written? If there is no date, are there any clues in the use of language?

- What is it saying?

- How is it being said?

- What questions do we need to ask to understand it?

From this point, you can then move into a more detailed discussion about the historical topic, theme, figure or period you are studying or introduce another relevant activity.

Exploring further

We hope that the lessons in this book will show you the power of working with archival material and will encourage you to integrate this approach into your history teaching with all your classes, regardless of the topics and themes you are covering. Once you have started teaching in this way, we hope that you will be encouraged to make use of your local archives and The National Archives as historians. There are countless sources in archives up and down the country that can open up your pupils' eyes to the past and bring history to life in your classroom.

The National Archives

The National Archives is home to more than 1,000 years of the nation's history. As the office archive and publisher for the UK government, and for England and Wales, its role is to preserve official government records for generations to come, and to make them accessible to all. From Shakespeare's will and Domesday Book to beautiful designs and photographs, its unique historical collection is one of the largest in the world.

fins.

Javel

at Tyburn about 1680.—From a contemporary print in the Edmund Gardne

How to use this book

Each lesson in this toolkit can be used to teach a specific topic, theme or requirement in the National Curriculum for history. The lessons are split into two sections: the first covers the National Curriculum for Key Stage 1 and the second focuses on the Key Stage 2 curriculum. The order in which you teach the lessons will depend on your scheme of work, so use the table of contents to dip in and out of each section to find a lesson that suits your needs.

The lessons are based on a single enquiry question that focuses on one or more original historical sources, mostly drawn from the collection at The National Archives. The lessons are split into three sections: a lesson overview, a lesson plan, and transcripts and worksheets.

⟳ Lesson overview

Each lesson plan begins with an overview featuring:

- **Lesson enquiry question:** Each lesson is based on a specific enquiry question that can be explored through one or more original historical sources.

- **Lesson focus:** The lesson focus clarifies exactly what your pupils will learn in the lesson, for example what they will be able to describe or explain by the end of the lesson. This section also explicitly links the lesson to the National Curriculum.

- **Resources required:** This section lists the resources you will need to run the lesson, including any sources, transcripts, worksheets and stationery.

- **Source(s):** An image of each source that will be used in the lesson is provided in the book for reference. A high-resolution, full-colour image of each source is available in the accompanying online resources at www.bloomsbury.com/primary-history-toolkit. Download the images you need ahead of the lesson and either project them on a whiteboard or print copies for pupils to share in their groups or pairs.

Lesson plan

Each lesson introduces three activities to help pupils explore the enquiry question:

- **Starter activity:** The lessons open with a starter activity that introduces pupils to the relevant topic or theme.

- **Main activity:** In the main activity, pupils engage with the source material to explore the enquiry question. Using questioning techniques and interactive activities, you can help pupils draw out the key information held within each source, form their own interpretations and use this to develop their understanding of the relevant curriculum content.

- **Creative activity:** The lessons conclude with a creative activity where pupils use their imaginations to bring history to life, whether that's by designing posters, writing letters or even baking bread! The creative activities are a great opportunity to link history to other subjects across the curriculum, including English, drama, art and design, and many more.

Transcripts and worksheets

Some of the written sources may be challenging for pupils to read, so we have included **transcripts** and **simplified transcripts** where necessary. These can be photocopied and handed out to pupils in the lesson. However, it's always best to let pupils observe the original source first, so they can make observations about its form and have a go at deciphering the text, before you hand out the transcript.

Where relevant, we have provided **worksheets** to support the lesson activities. These can be photocopied and handed out to pupils to complete.

Timings

We have not provided timings for the lesson plans, as these will depend on the context in which you are teaching. You may want to spend more time on certain activities and less on others according to the needs, abilities and interests of your pupils, and the requirements of your scheme of work. Each lesson plan does, however, provide a complete, fully rounded session on the relevant topic or theme.

Part 1
Key Stage 1

Introduction to Key Stage 1: Learning how to find out about the past

The lessons in this section are aimed at pupils in Key Stage 1 and can be used to build pupil confidence when working with primary evidence. They include employing the concept of 'the mystery document' outlined on page iv, using 'chat cards' to promote discussion, and developing observational skills and awareness of historical terms. Of course, these approaches work with older pupils too and we have continued to use them in our lessons for Key Stage 2.

The National Curriculum at Key Stage 1 requires pupils to develop an awareness of the past, learning common words and phrases to relate to the passing of time, asking and answering questions, and using stories and sources to understand about key historical figures, events and changes. Teaching historical significance is an important concept for the National Curriculum and using the historical sources in these lessons will allow pupils to explore how our memory of past events is constructed. Other ideas related to significance, for example innovation or impact of an event or person, which help contribute to pupils' understanding of the connection between past and present, can also be discussed.

The topics covered in the National Curriculum at Key Stage 1 are:

- changes within living memory
- events beyond living memory that are significant nationally or globally
- the lives of significant individuals in the past who have contributed to national and international achievements
- significant historical events, people and places in the pupils' own locality.

To support you in meeting these content requirements, in this section we have included lessons on seaside holidays, life in Victorian times, significant events, including the Great Fire of London, the sinking of the Titanic and the First World War, and significant individuals, including Queen Victoria, Walter Tull and Emily Davison. There is also a lesson on rural life, where you can explore with the pupils census data for your own region.

We hope the lessons in this section will help you bring the Key Stage 1 curriculum to life in your classroom.

Seaside holidays

⟳ Lesson overview

Lesson enquiry question

How have seaside holidays changed?

Resources required

Sources:

❶ Photograph of Bognor Beach.

❷ Photograph of children on the beach at Blackpool.

Lesson focus

Describe:

Describe what seaside holidays looked like in Victorian times.

Explain:

Explain how seaside holidays have changed in the past 150 years.

Curriculum link:

Changes within living memory.

❶ Bognor Beach.

❷ Children on the beach at Blackpool.

Copyright © Clare Horrie and Rachel Hillman, 2020

🚀 Starter activity

Talk to the pupils about holidays generally. You could ask them:

- What does a holiday mean?
- Where have you been on holiday?
- Who do you go with and what do you do on holiday?
- When do we have holidays?

Now focus in on the idea of a 'seaside' holiday and ask:

- Can you name any places by the sea?
- What types of things might you see, hear, touch or smell on a seaside holiday?
- What kinds of activities might you take part in at the seaside?

You could ask the pupils to act out little freeze-frames or mimes of activities on a seaside holiday, or even use a bag of sensory props to encourage discussion about some of the things that they might encounter on this type of holiday (for example shells and pebbles, sandpaper or moon sand for sand, the smell of vanilla essence for ice cream or the feel of an ice pack or water spray for the sea).

Next explain that they're going to find out what seaside holidays were like in the past when Queen Victoria was on the throne about 150 years ago. You can use images of Queen Victoria here and a timeline activity to help to start develop the pupils' understanding of chronology. A simple timeline with three or four marker images on it would be a good starting point, for example:

- a class picture of the pupils (to show today)
- man landing on the moon
- the sinking of the Titanic
- Queen Victoria.

✏️ Creative activity

Pupils could design a poster to advertise either a modern seaside holiday or a Victorian seaside holiday. Once they have finished, display the two sets of posters and discuss as a class the similarities and differences between the modern-day posters and the Victorian posters.

⭐ Main activity

Display the image of Bognor Beach on the whiteboard and use the spotlight tool or similar to focus in on different sections of the image.

Start by focussing in on one of the bathing machines. What do the pupils think this might be? Slowly move outwards from the bathing machine so that they can start to see the beach and the other bathing machines in the picture. Now ask them what they think these machines are for. Explain that they were used by rich Victorians to change into their bathing costumes and enter the sea.

Can the pupils spot anything else in the picture that can tell us about Victorian seaside holidays? If necessary, guide them towards the people paddling at the edge of the waves and the hotels in the background. You could also zoom in to look at some of the clothing that the figures on the beach are wearing.

Now explain to the pupils that they're going to look at another photograph of a Victorian seaside scene, and that this time they need to work in pairs as detectives, to see what else they can find out about seaside holidays at this time.

Give pupils a printed copy of the image showing children on the beach at Blackpool. They can draw and write their observations on the printed copy or just discuss in pairs. Ask them to look at and think about:

- who they can see on the beach
- how they are dressed
- what they are doing.

Once the pupils have had time to explore the image, bring them all back together to hear their findings.

Further questions to ask the class at this point could be:

- Are the children and grown-ups playing together? Why might this be?
- Why are the grown-ups fully dressed?
- Why are they holding umbrellas on such a hot day?

Now the pupils have made a number of observations about Victorian seaside holidays, ask them to think about what might be similar to seaside holidays today and what might be different. You could think about:

- the way in which grown-ups and children might interact on the beach today
- how we dress to have fun on the beach
- how we swim openly in the sea and how we might play in the sand.

Make a class list of these similarities and differences and you can then ask pupils to each draw a picture to illustrate one of these points.

Victorian toys

⊙ Lesson overview

Lesson enquiry question

What did children play with in Victorian times?

Resources required

Sources:

1. Dolls.
2. Design for spinning top.
3. Marbles game.
4. Hoop game.

Lesson focus

Describe:

Describe some of the toys that a Victorian child might have played with.

Explain:

Explain the similarities and differences between Victorian toys and toys today.

Curriculum link:

Changes within living memory.

1 Dolls.

3 Marbles game.

2 Design for spinning top.

4 Hoop game.

Copyright © Clare Horrie and Rachel Hillman, 2020

🚀 Starter activity

Talk to the pupils about their favourite toys. You could even arrange a time for them to bring a special toy into school to tell others about. The following questions might be useful:

- What is your favourite toy and why?
- Who do you play it with?
- If you could only use one word to describe your toy, what would it be?

Now show the pupils the source 'Dolls' on the whiteboard. Explain that this is a picture showing some children playing. Don't provide any further information at this stage. Give the pupils 20 seconds to look at the image before you remove it. What can they spot?

Once you've removed the image from the board, ask them to tell their partner about the different things that they remember seeing.

Now show the pupils the image again. What did they miss? Ask them to tell you about the things that they can see in the image. Suggested questions to ask could be:

- What are the different toys that you can spot?
- How are the children dressed?
- What else can you see in the room around the children?

Encourage the children to think about when this image was drawn. Does it show them toys or clothing that children would play with and wear today? How might this help us to work out when this picture was made?

Explain to the pupils that they are looking at an advert for an ABC game made during Victorian times about 150 years ago! You can use images of Queen Victoria here and the timeline activity described on page 3. Explain that children then, just like children today, would have loved playing with their toys and having fun with their friends. Lots of people were very poor and couldn't really afford many toys for their children. Ask the pupils if they think the children in the image are rich or poor. Why do they think this?

Explain that these children came from a very wealthy family and had some very expensive toys (for example the dolls' house, the doll and so on). Tell the pupils that they have found out about some of the toys that wealthy children might have played with in Victorian times from this source, but that they are now going to find out about some other popular toys.

⭐ Main activity

Give pupils copies of the three other sources and ask them to work in pairs or small groups. They will need to look carefully at the sources and try to work out the following things for each one:

- What can they see in the image?
- How do they think children would have played with this toy?
- Are there any toys like this today for children to play with?
- Do they think that the toy looks like fun? Why or why not?

Once the pupils have had time to explore all of the different images, bring them back together to hear their findings. Further questions to ask or focus on as a whole class could be:

- Are any of these toys similar to the toys we play with today?
- Are any of these toys very different to the toys we play with today? How are they different?
- Which toys do you think would be most fun to play with: toys today or toys from Victorian times? Why do you think this?

Now that the pupils have made a number of observations about Victorian toys, ask them to think about toys today and any other more specific similarities or differences between them and Victorian toys. Scribe a class list to record their ideas.

You could also talk further to the pupils about the types of toys and games that very poor children would have played with and how these compare to today's pastimes.

✏️ Creative activity

Pupils could design their own poster to advertise a Victorian toy of their choice. To support this activity, you could get hold of some simple replica Victorian toys and the children could spend some time playing with these and deciding which is their favourite and why. Their poster could then be an advert for their chosen toy.

Victorian schools

⟳ Lesson overview

Lesson enquiry question

How has school changed since Victorian times?

Resources required

Sources:

❶ Plan of Quatt School.

❷ Photograph of pupils from Eddlestone School, 1899.

❸ Ups and Downs of School Life.

Other:

• Worksheet: School rooms. Photocopy one worksheet per group and cut them up into individual cards.

Lesson focus

Describe:

Describe what a Victorian school was like.

Explain:

Explain the similarities and differences between a Victorian school and a school today.

Curriculum link:

Changes within living memory.

❶ Plan of Quatt School.

❷ Photograph of pupils from Eddlestone School, 1899.

❸ Ups and Downs of School Life.

Copyright © Clare Horrie and Rachel Hillman, 2020

🚀 Starter activity

Talk to the pupils about the layout of their school. You could ask them:

- What rooms and outdoor spaces are there?
- What are the spaces used for?
- What would a plan of their school tell a visitor about the different subjects they study and the ways in which they learn?

You could get hold of a plan of your school to help.

Now show the pupils the plan of Quatt School on the whiteboard. Without giving any details about the school itself, explain that they are going to pretend to be visitors to this school and have to find out as much as possible from studying the plan in small groups.

Give each group a printed copy of the Quatt School plan and a set of cards from the worksheet. Can they put the pictures in the right places on the plan to show what the rooms are used for? Are there any rooms that they're not sure about the purpose of?

Ask the pupils to feed back on what they've found out. Sort their observations into a table of similarities and differences between Quatt School and their own school. Why are there so many differences? Is this plan showing a school today? If not, when do they think this plan was created? Why do they think this?

Explain that they are looking at a plan for a school during Victorian times about 150 years ago! You can use images of Queen Victoria and the timeline activity from page 3 here to develop pupils' understanding of chronology. Explain that learning was very different then, with boys and girls studying different subjects in separate classrooms. They even had separate playgrounds and entrances!

You could use a sensory bag of props here to introduce further information about Victorian schooling, for example slate (for writing), an abacus (for counting), an inkwell (older children would use a pen and inkwell to write in a copybook), three wooden or plastic letter Rs to represent the 'three Rs' (wRiting, Reading, aRithmetic) and a Bible (teaching of religion was very important).

✏️ Creative activity

Pupils could design their own posters for the 'Ups and Downs of School Life' today. What would they choose to represent? When the pupils have completed their posters, discuss as a class the similarities and differences between their modern-day posters and the Victorian version.

⭐ Main activity

Display the photograph of Eddlestone School, 1899 on the whiteboard. Ask the pupils to look carefully at the picture for a minute before asking them to feed back on the following things. You could annotate the photograph on the whiteboard as they feed back their answers.

- What can you see in the image?
- How are the children dressed? Are they wearing the sorts of clothes that children wear today? If not, what's different about their clothing?
- Are all the people in the photograph children? Can you spot the man? Who do you think he is?
- Where do you think the children are?
- Why do you think that the children have had their photograph taken?

Explain that this is a photograph taken at a school in Victorian times and that the man in the centre is the teacher. This is quite a small school, but some classes could be very big, so teachers would be helped by some of the older children (monitors) to deliver the teaching.

Now explain to the pupils that they're going to look at another image about a Victorian school, and that they need to work in pairs as detectives to see what else they can find out about Victorian schools. Give each pair a copy of the image 'Ups and Down of School Life'. They can draw or write their observations on the image. Ask them to look at and think about:

- what they can see in each picture and what the children are doing
- how the children are dressed
- why they think it's called the 'Ups and Downs of School Life'.

Once the pupils have had time to explore the image, bring them all back together to hear their findings. Further questions to ask or focus on as a class could be:

- Why is the child in the first image wearing the paper hat? This is the dunce's hat. Children who had got something incorrect or had misbehaved were forced to wear it as they stood in the corner in shame. You could talk about the unkindness of this method, how everyone struggles with different things, and that today we encourage and help children to learn. You could also talk further about punishments in Victorian schools, for example the cane and writing lines.
- Where are the children ice skating? This was a common pastime when the lakes and rivers froze and was a good way for children to be active. They didn't have PE but would have 'drill', which involved stretches and running.

Now ask pupils to revisit the list of similarities and differences they made between Quatt School and their own school in the starter activity. Would they add anything?

✏️ Worksheet: School rooms

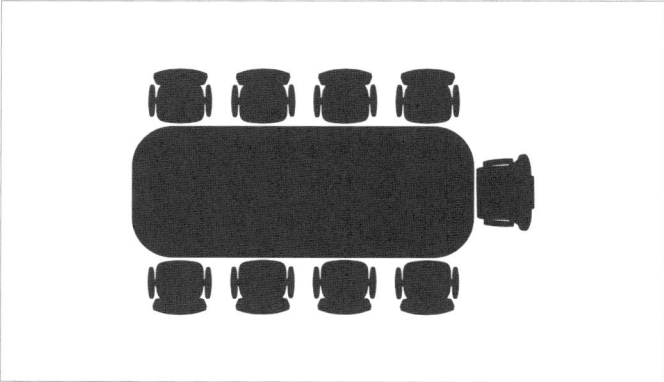

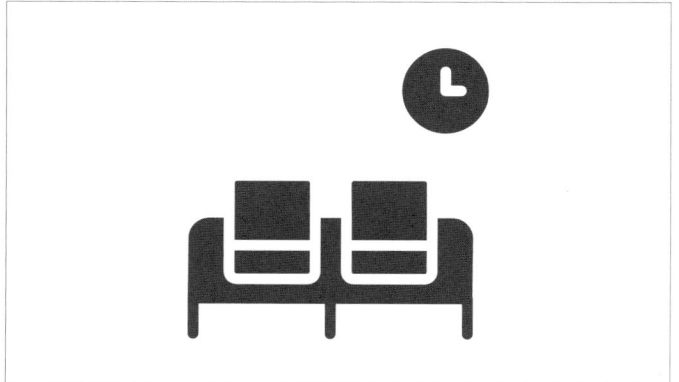

Copyright © Clare Horrie and Rachel Hillman, 2020

Great Fire of London: What happened?

⟲ Lesson overview

Lesson enquiry question

What happened in the Great Fire of London?

Resources required

Sources:

❶ Wenceslas Hollar's survey map of London with focus on the illustration.

Other:

- Story bag with simple props, such as a crown, a feely bag with leather, wool and wax candles, a nightcap and orange voile.
- Mini whiteboards.

Lesson focus

Describe:

Describe two or three facts about what happened during the Great Fire of London.

Explain:

Explain why the fire spread so quickly.

Curriculum link:

Events beyond living memory that are significant nationally or globally.

HOLLAR'S "EXACT SURVEIGH" OF THE CITY OF LONDON, 1667

❶ Wenceslas Hollar's survey map of London with focus on the illustration.

🚀 Starter activity

Display the extracted image from the survey map on the whiteboard and allow pupils to look at the image for ten seconds only. Then cover the image and ask them to chat with a partner about what they saw or noticed in those ten seconds.

Hear some of their ideas and then show the pupils the image again, this time with no time constraints. What did they miss the first time around? Use the following prompts to help if necessary:

- What additional things can you see?
- What do you think is happening in the picture?
- Why do you think this?

⭐ Main activity

Explain to pupils that this image shows an event that happened in London a long time ago called the Great Fire of London. It was drawn by someone who was alive at the time and saw the fire with their own eyes. Here you can use a timeline, making jumps of around 100 years, to introduce pupils to the 17th century and to 1666, the year of the Great Fire. In the timeline, you could include an event that the children are familiar with, such as the year they started school, before adding events beyond their living memory, such as the beginning of the First World War (1914), the start of Queen Victoria's reign (1837), the French Revolution (1789) and the union of Scotland and England (1707). Include several events in the 1600s to introduce the 17th century and what was happening at the time, including the Great Fire of London (1666), the Great Plague (1665) and the ascent of Charles II to the throne (1660).

Using a story bag with simple props, introduce pupils to the events of that day. Use images of Stuart London and the types of buildings that existed to set context and to help pupils understand what the buildings were made from and why the fire was able to spread so quickly. A suggested script and list of props is included below.

Storytelling script introducing the Great Fire of London

Props required:

- crown
- feely bag with leather, wool and wax candles
- nightcap
- orange voile.

Introduce King Charles II, King of England and Scotland at this time. A pupil could play the role of Charles (use a crown to signify his status), and you can explain how he was known as the 'Merry Monarch'. Ask pupils why they think this was. Explain that King Charles II liked to entertain and have parties, and hold a lively court. You could ask the pupils to all pretend that they are members of King Charles's court and are having a wonderful time at one of his parties. Get them to freeze-frame in a party position!

Explain that at this time, London was very different to the city that we know today. There were no cars, no cinemas and no trains! But it was still a big city, even then, with lots of people living and working there. Ask the pupils what sorts of jobs they think people might have had then. Introduce a feely bag of different materials at this point, with some leather, some wool and a wax candle. Get the pupils to explore what's in the bag. Explain that people might have worked as leather workers (using leather to make shoes, purses and so on), as weavers (using wool to make cloth), and as chandlers (making and selling candles). Ask the pupils why they think candles were so important at this time. What were they used for?

  Copyright © Clare Horrie and Rachel Hillman, 2020

Explain that people in the 1600s didn't have electricity, so they used candles for light and used fires to heat their homes and to cook on. Explain that people lived so closely together in London at this time, they could reach out their window and shake hands with their neighbour next door. Get the pupils to all shake hands with their neighbours to get a sense of this. What would it have been like living so closely together? (It would certainly have been noisy, smelly and very overcrowded.)

Now introduce Thomas Farrinor. Ask a pupil to play Thomas and explain that he's a baker who makes bread for people to buy. He also makes puddings, but not the sweet puddings we eat today. These were puddings filled with suet and cheap cuts of meat! Get all of the pupils to pretend that they've just bitten into one of these puddings. What do they think? Ask them to show delighted or disgusted expressions as they eat their pudding!

Explain that Thomas Farrinor has finished work for the day and he's about to go to bed. Give the pupil a nightcap to wear and ask them to pat down all of the ashes in the fire to make sure that the oven is well and truly put out. Then Thomas goes off to bed (give the pupil a candle to light their way through their home and upstairs to bed).

But, something very bad is about to happen. Get all of the pupils to look very scared! A spark from the fire is still alight and it has fallen onto the floor, which is covered in sacking, and started to burn! Ask another pupil to play Thomas Farrinor's maid. She notices the fire first, so get the pupil to shout, 'Fire, fire!' All of the pupils can then pass this on to the next person in the circle, so that all of the neighbours know that a fire is spreading.

Use an orange voile or similar to show the fire spreading from house to house. Explain to the pupils that as the houses were built so closely together, it was very easy for the fire to spread and spread quickly. Pupils could get into groups of four, with two of them making an arch to represent a building and the other two pupils can be the flames.

Ask the pupils how they think the fire was put out. Were there fire engines and fire brigades like we have today? Explain that the streets were very narrow and that water had to be taken from the River Thames to the site of the fire. This was done by people forming long lines and passing buckets of water along the line. Ask the pupils to pretend to pass the water along. What would have been the problem with this method? (It takes a long time.)

Explain that the fire burnt from Sunday 2nd September to Thursday 6th September. Over a third of London had been destroyed by the flames.

Once the story is over, refer back to some of the images used in the Hollar map to describe the fire.

Ask pupils what they think it might have been like for people witnessing the fire. What might they have heard, seen, smelt and touched? Now in pairs or small groups, can the pupils choose five adjectives (describing words) to sum up what it might have been like to witness the fire? Ask them to write these on their mini whiteboards to share and discuss with others in the class.

🖊 Creative activity

In small groups, ask the pupils to prepare a mini freeze-frame of a section of the story about the events of the Great Fire. This could be, for example:

- the fire spreading quickly from house to house
- people escaping the fire by crossing the river
- attempts to put the fire out by using buckets of water passed along lines of people.

Once the pupils have planned what they are going to do, ask each group to perform their freeze-frame in turn. During the performance, the other groups observe the freeze-frame and work out which part of the story it's depicting and what exactly is happening.

Great Fire of London: How do we know what happened?

⟳ Lesson overview

Lesson enquiry question

How do we know what happened in the Great Fire of London?

Resources required

Sources:

❶ Wenceslas Hollar's survey map of London with focus on the illustration.

❷ The hearth tax return for Pudding Lane.

❸ Agas map.

Other:

- Transcript for source 2.
- Worksheet: Key facts. Photocopy one per pupil.

Lesson focus

Describe:

Describe two or three facts about what happened during the Great Fire of London.

Explain:

Explain what each document tells us about the Great Fire and whether it supports the historians' account.

Curriculum link:

Events beyond living memory that are significant nationally or globally.

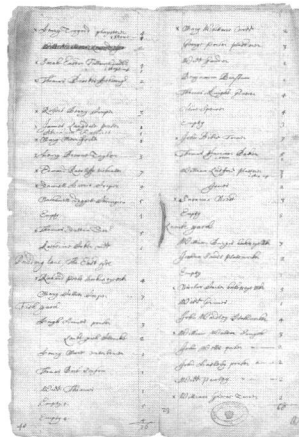

❶ Wenceslas Hollar's survey map of London with focus on the illustration.

❷ The hearth tax return for Pudding Lane.

❸ Agas map.

   Copyright © Clare Horrie and Rachel Hillman, 2020

🚀 Starter activity

This lesson uses three sources that historians have used to find out about the Great Fire of London.

First, recap with the pupils what they can remember about the Great Fire from the previous lesson, including what happened, where the fire started and why.

Explain that you're now going to show them a source that was made around the time of the Great Fire of London. Display the full image of Wenceslas Hollar's survey map on the whiteboard. Ask the pupils whether they recognise anything. If they look carefully, they should be able to spot the image of the fire that they looked at in Lesson 1 (page 9). Ask them what else they see now that they can look at the full source.

Give pupils five minutes to work in pairs or small groups to discuss what else they can see on the document. Ask pupils to feed back their ideas about the following:

- What type of document is this? (It's a map.)
- How can they tell? (You can see street names, buildings and a key.)
- Why are there not many buildings shown in the large white area of the map? (Most of the buildings in this area were destroyed in the fire.)
- What does this tell us?

Explain to the pupils that they now know about the story of the Great Fire of London, but how have they found out this information? Where has this information come from? Once the class have offered some answers, explain about buildings called archives, which look after documents created at the time of the Great Fire. These help historians to find out what happened and why. Tell the pupils that their task today is to look at some of these documents and to check whether historians have used this evidence properly. Have they got the story of the Great Fire correct?

✒️ Creative activity

Pupils could make a poster or zine (a mini magazine) about the different types of documents that they've looked at to find out about the Great Fire. You could print off small versions of the documents for pupils to cut up and stick on their zines, and hand out copies of the 'fact bank' on page 15 to help.

⭐ Main activity

Ask the pupils if they can remember where the fire started (Pudding Lane). Now ask what type of document we could look at to see if there really was a Pudding Lane in 1666. Guide the pupils' answers back to Hollar's map.

Hollar's map

Hand out copies of the map for pupils to look at in detail.

- Can you find the famous building on the map that the fire didn't reach? (The Tower of London.)
- Can you find London Bridge? (London Bridge was the first landmark to burn in the fire. Next to London Bridge was a giant water wheel that collected buckets of water from the Thames. People called water-bearers used these buckets to put out fires. The water wheel was destroyed in the fire.)
- Can pupils find Pudding Lane?
- Was there a Pudding Lane in 1666?
- What else did you learn from looking at the map?

Hearth tax return

Ask pupils where on Pudding Lane the historians say the fire started (in Thomas Farrinor's bakery). Now ask them what type of document we could look at to see if Thomas Farrinor lived on Pudding Lane in 1666. Accept their responses before introducing the hearth tax return. Explain that the source shows everyone who lived in different parts of London and who owned an oven and/or a fireplace (hearth) in their homes. This was because they were charged money (tax) by the King for every hearth and oven. As Thomas Farrinor ran a bakery, his name should be on this list. Look at the document as a class and read the headings. Pupils then work on the following tasks in groups. Share the transcript if needed.

- Can you find Thomas Farrinor?
- How many ovens and hearths did he have?
- What did the other people on the street do for a living?
- Is there anyone who has a job you don't recognise?

Agas map

Ask pupils whether many people died in the Great Fire. Why not? Where do historians say they escaped to? Introduce the Agas map and hand out printed copies. Explain that it was originally made of wood about 60 years before the fire. Discuss the following with the pupils:

- How would people have escaped the fire?
- Can you find any water-bearers like Henry Moore? Why weren't they able to put out the fire?
- Were the historians right in saying that people were able to escape the fire? How did they do this?

Ask pupils about the different types of documents that they've looked at in this lesson. Based on this evidence, do they think the historians have got the story about the Great Fire of London correct? Why? What have pupils learnt today that they didn't already know?

Transcript

Pudding Lane Hearth Tax Return

Mary Whittacre widow	2
George Porter plasterer	3
Widdow Gander	1
Benjamin Burstow	1
Thomas Knight glasier [glass maker]	4
Alice Spencer	4
Empty	3
John Bibie turner [person who works with a turning lathe, a tool for shaping and cutting wood – important in making barrels]	3
Thomas Farrinor baker 1 oven	5 1
William Ludford plasterer 1 stop up	3 1
Jones	2
Susanna Noest	3
Empty	3
Lanbe Yard	
William Burgis hook & eye maker	3
Joshua Sands plateworker	2
Empty	3
Nicolas Carter hook & eye maker	5
Widdow Grimes	1
John Wardley clothworker	4
William Walter smyth [blacksmith who worked with metal and made horseshoes]	3
John Wells porter	2
John Hasleby porter	2
Widdow Pawley	2
William Greene turner	2
	68

Copyright © Clare Horrie and Rachel Hillman, 2020

📝 Worksheet: Key facts

Here are some key facts about what happened during the Great Fire of London in 1666.

- The fire started in Pudding Lane, in the shop of the King's baker, Thomas Farrinor.

- The fire destroyed one third of the city of London.

- The fire began on the morning of 2nd September 1666.

- London Bridge and St Paul's Cathedral were both burnt in the fire.

- King Charles II ordered that shops and houses should be pulled down to stop the fire from spreading.

- 100,000 people were made homeless by the fire.

- Thomas Farrinor did not put out the fire that heated his oven. Sparks from the oven fell onto dry flour sacks covering the floor. This is what started the Great Fire of London.

- Water-bearers helped to put out the fire.

- Lots of people left the city whilst it was burning. Some people even buried their belongings to save them from the fire.

Great Fire of London: How was London rebuilt?

⟳ Lesson overview

Lesson enquiry question

How was London rebuilt after the Great Fire of London?

Resources required

Sources:

❶ Charles II's declaration to London following the Great Fire.

❷ Image of St Paul's Cathedral.

Other:

- Collection of craft materials, including cardboard, mini boxes, felt tips and colouring pencils.
- Worksheet: Design a new building. Photocopy one per pupil.

Lesson focus

Describe:

Describe two or three facts about what happened during the Great Fire of London.

Explain:

Explain why the fire spread so quickly.

Curriculum link:

Events beyond living memory that are significant nationally or globally.

In the first place the woful experience in this late heavy visitation hath sufficiently convinced all men of the pernicious consequences which have attended the building with Timber, and even with Stone it self, and the notable benefit of Brick, which in so many places hath resisted and even extinguished the Fire; And we do therefore hereby declare Our express Wil and Pleasure, That no man whatsoever shal presume to erect any House or Building, great or smal, but of Brick, or Stone, and if any man shal do the contrary, the next Magistrate shal forthwith cause it to be pulled down,

all other eminent and notorious Streets, shal be of such a breadth, as may with Gods blessing prevent the mischief that one side may suffer if the other be on fire,

nor wil we suffer any Lanes or Allyes to be erected, but whereupon mature deliberation the same shal be found absolutely necessary,

no house shall be erected within so many foot of the River,

any houses to be inhabited by Brewers, or Diers, or Sugar-Bakers, which Trades by their continual Smoaks contribute very much to the unhealthiness of the adjacent places; but We require the Lord Major and Aldermen of *London* upon a full consideration, and weighing all conveniences and inconveniences that can be foreseen, to propose such a place as may be fit for all those Trades which are carried on by smoak to inhabit together,

❶ Charles II's declaration to London following the Great Fire.

Copyright © Clare Horrie and Rachel Hillman, 2020

🚀 Starter activity

Show the pupils the image of King Charles II's declaration to London following the Great Fire. Explain that he hoped to improve the city and prevent another fire. His declaration (you can define this as instructions or orders) gave people information about how London was to be rebuilt. It was hung all around London.

You could read the declaration aloud to the pupils, and also give them an image of the declaration to look at. Discuss the following as a class:

- What is the declaration telling people?
- Why is it telling people not to build their homes out of wood?

Explain to the pupils that one of the buildings that was rebuilt from stone is very famous and still stands in London today. It was designed by a very famous architect called Christopher Wren. Ask the pupils whether they know what the building is called.

Show the pupils the image of St Paul's rebuilt, and explain that this new St Paul's was designed to impress everyone who saw it. King Charles II was using the occasion of the Great Fire as an opportunity to make some of London's buildings even more exciting and impressive to look at.

⭐ Main activity

Explain to the pupils that they are now going to be architects just like Christopher Wren! They've been asked to design some new buildings for London today, so that it can be even bigger and even better than ever before!

Give each pupil a planning sheet in preparation for designing their own building (you can use the worksheet on page 18). They will need to think about what their building will be used for. Will it be a church, palace, place of entertainment, hotel or museum? They will also need to come up with a name for their building. Finally, they should describe three key features that they want to include in their design and explain why they've chosen them. Perhaps it will be painted in a bright colour to stand out, for example, or it will have a tall tower so that the building has views across London.

✏️ Creative activity

Give the pupils a selection of craft materials, such as cardboard, mini boxes, felt tips, colouring pencils and stickers, and ask them to build their building.

When the pupils have finished building, you could create a large floor map of London, so that all the pupils can place their finished buildings on the map to display their impressive vision of London!

2 Image of St Paul's Cathedral.

Copyright © Clare Horrie and Rachel Hillman, 2020

✏️ Worksheet: Design a new building

Design a new building for London, so that the city is bigger and better than ever before. Use this sheet to plan your new building.

What will your building be used for? Will it be a church, a palace, a hotel or something else?

What will your building be called?

Describe three features your building will have. Why have you chosen them?

Feature	Why have you chosen it?
1.	
2.	
3.	

What will your building look like? Draw your building below.

Copyright © Clare Horrie and Rachel Hillman, 2020

Jubilee Victoria: What happened?

⊙ Lesson overview

Lesson enquiry question

What happened at Queen Victoria's Diamond Jubilee and how can we find out?

Resources required

Sources:

❶ Photograph of Bank House Club decorated for Queen Victoria's Diamond Jubilee 1897, Dartford, Kent.

❷ Photograph that shows a crowd gathered to celebrate Queen Victoria's Diamond Jubilee after her 60-year reign, 22nd June 1897, Alston, Cumberland.

Other:

- Question sheet: Using photographs to find out about the past. Photocopy enough for pupils to share one sheet in pairs or small groups.
- Worksheet: Design a postcard. Photocopy one for each pupil.

Lesson focus

Describe:

Describe how Queen Victoria's reign was celebrated and use the photographs to infer more about life in Victorian times. These photographs come from a time when people first started to take photographs with simple cameras.

Explain:

Explain that the photographs concern Queen Victoria's Diamond Jubilee, marking a reign of 60 years in 1897.

Curriculum link:

Events beyond living memory that are significant nationally or globally.

❶ Photograph of Bank House Club decorated for Queen Victoria's Diamond Jubilee 1897, Dartford, Kent.

🚀 Starter activity

Show the whole class the first source (the photograph of Bank House Club) to get them thinking about the subject. Display the photograph on the whiteboard and ask pupils the following:

- What can you see?
- What do the words mean?
- Whose reign is it?
- Why does the building have flags?

Explain the term 'diamond jubilee' and tell the pupils that the photograph depicts a building that is decorated to celebrate Queen Victoria's Diamond Jubilee in 1897.

✏️ Creative activity

Ask pupils to make a postcard celebrating the 60-year reign of Queen Victoria. First, they design a decorative image for the front of their postcard. This can then be supplemented with a creative writing activity, where pupils imagine they have attended a celebration for Queen Victoria's Jubilee and are writing to tell their friends about the celebration. The postcards can be cut out and stuck together to create a frieze for the wall. You can use the worksheet on page 22 as a handout for this activity.

To support this activity, provide pupils with access to appropriate topic books and pictures on Queen Victoria or take a look at this website: www.nationalarchives.gov.uk/victorians.

⭐ Main activity

Divide the class into small groups and give each group a copy of the second source (the photograph of the crowd gathered in Cumberland) and some sugar paper. Ask them to put themselves in the photograph and consider the following questions as a group:

- What can you see?
- What can you hear?
- What would you feel (physically)?
- How would you feel (emotionally)?

Now discuss these questions together as a class:

- How is the photograph composed?
- What is the message of the photograph?
- Why has it been taken?
- How historically significant is it? What does it say it about Queen Victoria or life in Victorian times?
- How would you rank your findings from the most significant to the least significant?

Give each group a copy of the question sheet about photographs as sources on page 21. Ask them to discuss the questions together.

❷ Photograph that shows a crowd gathered to celebrate Queen Victoria's Diamond Jubilee after her 60-year reign, 22nd June 1897, Alston, Cumberland.

Copyright © Clare Horrie and Rachel Hillman, 2020

📝 Question sheet: Using photographs to find out about the past

Take another look at the photograph showing the crowd celebrating Queen Victoria's Diamond Jubilee. Think about these questions in your groups.

1. Where is this photograph taken?

2. Why might this photograph have been taken?

3. Who might have seen the photograph?

4. What can you see?

5. What does the photograph tell you about:

• Queen Victoria

• children's lives

• clothing

• shopping

• houses?

6. Do you think the photograph is posed?

7. If you think it is, does that make it less important for finding out about the past?

8. What other types of sources could help us to find out more about Queen Victoria's Jubilee?

✍ Worksheet: Design a postcard

Design a postcard that celebrates Queen Victoria's Diamond Jubilee.

Now imagine you have attended a celebration for Queen Victoria's Diamond Jubilee. On the back of your postcard, write to a friend to describe the celebration.

Copyright © Clare Horrie and Rachel Hillman, 2020

Jubilee Victoria:
How did the Queen celebrate?

⊙ Lesson overview

Lesson enquiry question

How did the Queen celebrate her Diamond Jubilee?

Resources required

Sources:

❶ An invitation to Buckingham Palace for local government officials, 23rd June 1897.

❷ An official engagement book, 21st June 1897.

Lesson focus

Describe:

Describe how Queen Victoria's reign was celebrated through the use of formal invitations and an engagement book.

Explain:

Explain that the sources concern Queen Victoria's Diamond Jubilee, marking a reign of 60 years in 1897.

Curriculum link:

Events beyond living memory that are significant nationally or globally.

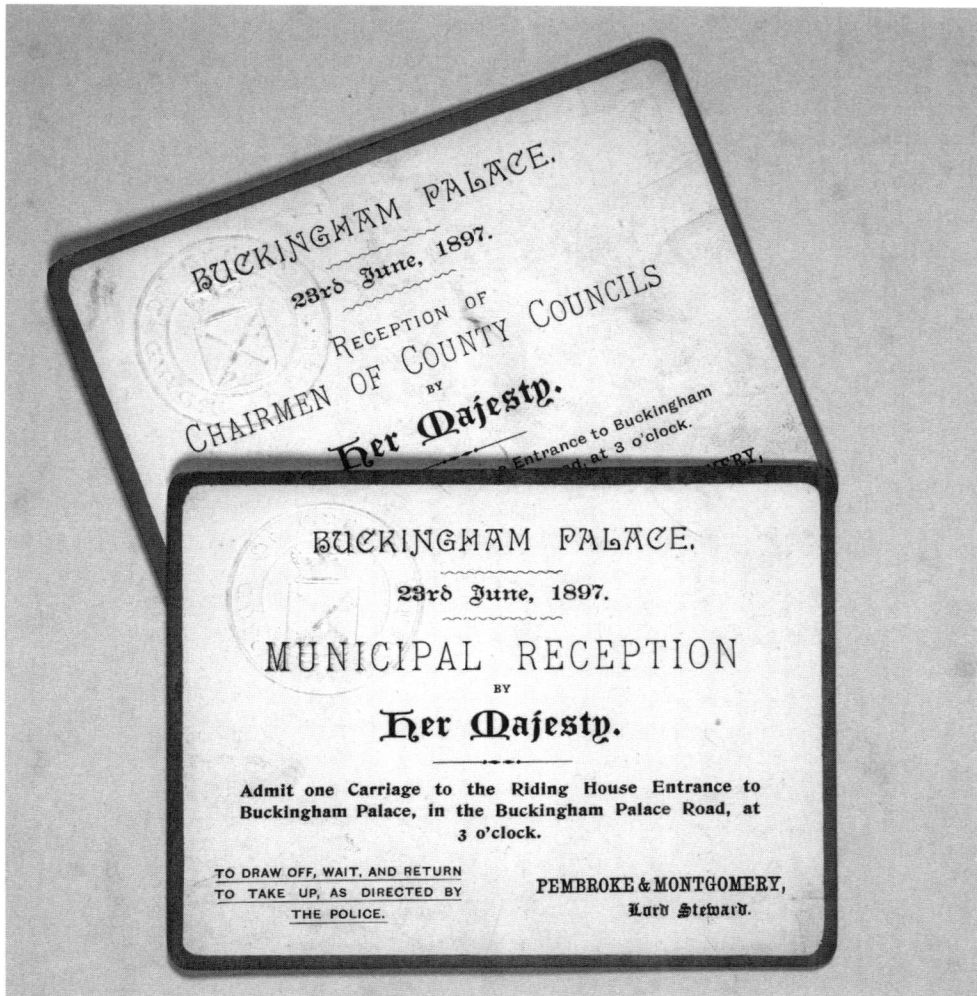

❶ An invitation to Buckingham Palace for local government officials, 23rd June 1897.

Copyright © Clare Horrie and Rachel Hillman, 2020

🚀 Starter activity

Show the pupils the first source (an invitation to Buckingham Palace) as a mystery document (see page iv). Display it on the whiteboard or hand out printed copies before discussing with them the following:

- What is this source?
- Where is the event taking place?
- When is it taking place?
- Who has been invited?
- What does the source tell us about how things were organised for the Jubilee? Help pupils to think about the plans for carriages, the fact that police would have been there to control crowds and that the invitation is printed, which suggests a lot of people have been invited.
- Why would this be an important event?

✏️ Creative activity

Encourage pupils to find out about women's evening dress in the late 19th century. They can then make a poster with a labelled diagram to show what men and women wore as evening dress in Victorian times.

⭐ Main activity

Show the whole class the second source (the official engagement book). Hand out printed versions of the source so pupils can study them in groups and discuss these questions:

- What can you see?
- What does it describe?
- Whose reign is it?
- What is the date?
- Who are the guests?
- What does this tell us about how powerful Britain was at that time?
- Why is this source printed?

Make sure you explain the term 'Levée dress': dark uniform, including a three-cornered hat with feather trimming, tail coat with buttons showing the Victorian Royal Arms, a pair of trousers with a broad stripe and a waistcoat. 'Full dress' for the evening meant wearing a white waistcoat and tie with a black tailcoat and trousers for men. You should also define: banquet, reception, colonial and imperial.

Bring the class back together and invite pupils to share their findings. Conclude the activity by discussing the question: 'What is the significance of this source?'

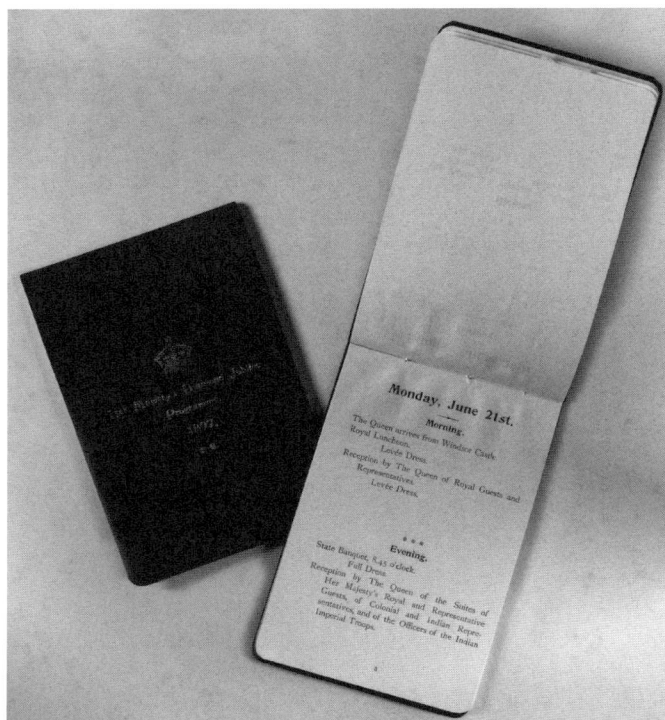

❷ An official engagement book, 21st June 1897.

Copyright © Clare Horrie and Rachel Hillman, 2020

Jubilee Victoria: How did the people celebrate?

↻ Lesson overview

Lesson enquiry question

How did the people celebrate Queen Victoria's Diamond Jubilee?

Resources required

Sources:

❶ Souvenir poster.

❷ Queen Victoria in carriage procession, London, 1897.

❸ Queen Victoria Diamond Jubilee bonfire, Chippenham, Wiltshire.

Lesson focus

Describe:

Describe how Queen Victoria's reign was celebrated through the use of a souvenir poster and photographs.

Explain:

Explain that the sources concern Queen Victoria's Diamond Jubilee, marking a reign of 60 years in 1897.

Curriculum link:

Events beyond living memory that are significant nationally or globally.

❷ Queen Victoria in carriage procession, London, 1897.

❶ Souvenir poster.

🚀 Starter activity

Show pupils the first source (the souvenir poster) by displaying it on the whiteboard. Explain that this was a souvenir poster for the Diamond Jubilee and define the term 'souvenir'. Discuss with the class the following:

- What type of source is this?
- How has the source shown Queen Victoria?
- What does the source tell us about some of her children?
- What does the source tell us about Victoria's life as queen?
- What does the poster tell us about the power of Britain then?
- Why was this poster produced?

⭐ Main activity

Now show the whole class both of the remaining sources (the photographs of Queen Victoria in carriage procession and of the Diamond Jubilee bonfire). Compare and contrast the two photographs as a class. Use the following prompts:

- What can you see?
- What are the people doing?
- How are the photographs different?
- What is the significance of these photographs?
- Which photograph is more useful for finding out about the Jubilee? Can you explain why?

✏️ Creative activity

Ask pupils to make a collection of pictures and souvenirs showing how events in the lives of our royal family today have been celebrated, for example royal weddings, births or anniversaries. How similar or different are they from how Queen Victoria's Diamond Jubilee was celebrated?

❸ Queen Victoria Diamond Jubilee bonfire, Chippenham, Wiltshire.

Copyright © Clare Horrie and Rachel Hillman, 2020

Titanic: What was life like on-board?

Lesson overview

Lesson enquiry question

What was life like on-board the Titanic?

Resources required

Sources:

1 Emergency telegram.

2 RMS Titanic at Belfast.

3 Image of first-class bedroom.

4 Image of lounge.

5 Image of gym.

6 Image of third-class berth.

Other:

· Worksheet: Write a postcard. Photocopy one per pupil.
· Question sheet. Photocopy one per pair.

Lesson focus

Describe:

Describe two or three facts about the Titanic and what happened to it.

Explain:

Explain some of the differences between first-class and third-class travel.

Curriculum link:

Significant historical events, people and places in pupils' own locality.

1 Emergency telegram.

2 RMS Titanic at Belfast.

3 Image of first-class bedroom. (Public domain.)

4 Image of lounge. (Public domain.)

5 Image of gym. (Public domain.)

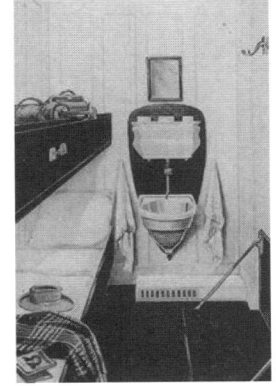

6 Image of third-class berth. (Public domain.)

Copyright © Clare Horrie and Rachel Hillman, 2020

🚀 Starter activity

Display the image of the emergency telegram on the whiteboard. Before giving any information about the source, ask the pupils to take a few minutes just to look at the document and then feed back on the things that they can see. Possible questions that you could ask include:

- How has this document been made – has it been handwritten, drawn or typed?
- What type of document could it be? Does it look like a letter with lots of long sentences or is the information in much shorter sections?
- Are there any words or names that the pupils recognise? (They should be able to spot 'Titanic' and 'SOS'.)
- What is this document telling people about what has happened?

Explain to the pupils that this is an emergency telegram that was sent by a ship called the Titanic in 1912 (over 100 years ago!). Ask the pupils if any of them have heard about the Titanic before and what happened to it.

Explain that an emergency telegram (radio telegram) was a message sent between two ships at sea, so they could communicate with each other. There would be a receiver set (to receive messages) and a transmitter set (to send messages) on-board ships that had this technology.

Explain that the Titanic had to use this messaging system when it hit an iceberg on its maiden voyage across the Atlantic. This ship had been described as the most luxurious and impressive ship of its kind. Some had even called it 'unsinkable'. Yet late on the evening of 14th April, it hit an iceberg and sank in less than three hours. Only 705 people were rescued from the 2,200 on-board.

Point out some of the other interesting coding on the telegram:

- CQD means 'All stations: distress'.
- MGY is the code name for the Titanic.
- SS Birma is the Russian ship in the vicinity to receive messages from the Titanic.

✏️ Creative activity

Pupils could write a short postcard about their experiences as a first-class passenger on-board the Titanic. You can photocopy and hand out the worksheet on page 30 to support this activity.

⭐ Main activity

Explain that in this lesson pupils are going to find out more about life on-board the Titanic before disaster struck. As a class, you could put together a list of questions about things the pupils would like to find out. For example:

- Can we find out the names of any of the passengers on-board?
- What was the accommodation like for people travelling on the ship?
- What types of entertainment were there for people on-board?

Introduce pupils to the idea of different classes of travel. Explain that passengers could travel in first, second or third class. The richest people on-board would have travelled in first class and the poorest in third class.

Display the photograph of the Titanic at Belfast and ask pupils for their impressions of the ship. Discuss its size and how luxurious it was for the time. Give each pupil a 'first-class ticket' and explain that they are going to be using documents to find out what it was like being a first-class passenger on-board the ship.

Split the class into pairs and hand each pair a copy of the photographs of the first-class bedroom, the lounge and the gym, as well as a copy of the question sheet on page 29. Using the question sheet, ask the pupils to investigate each photograph to find out what it reveals about life for first-class passengers.

Once the pupils have had an opportunity to look at the different images of first-class accommodation, bring them back together to feed back as a class. What did they notice about the rooms that first-class passengers could use? What do these rooms tell us about the types of entertainment the first-class passengers had on-board?

You can share the following information with pupils. First-class passengers had access to the gym, including an electric horse, rowing machine and cycling machines. First-class passengers' accommodation varied from several lavishly decorated state rooms with their own sitting room, private bedrooms, parlour rooms and private bathrooms, down to a single person's large room with a bed, sofa, dressing table and washbasin.

Now show the pupils the image of the third-class cabin. As a class, ask them the following questions:

- What can they see?
- What differences are there between the first- and third-class cabins?
- Which class would they have preferred to travel and why?

Copyright © Clare Horrie and Rachel Hillman, 2020

✎ Question sheet: Using photographs to find out about the past

First-class lounge

Look at the photograph of the first-class lounge. Now answer the questions.

1. What can you see?

_____

2. How can you tell it was designed for the rich passengers?

_____

3. What type of room is this?

_____

4. What do you think it was used for?

_____

Gymnasium

Look at the photograph of the gymnasium. Now answer the questions.

1. What can you see?

_____

2. What do you think this room was used for?

_____

First-class cabin

Look at the photograph of the first-class cabin. Now answer the questions.

1. What can you see?

_____

2. What do you think this room was used for?

_____

3. How can you tell it was designed for the richer passengers on-board?

_____

✍ Worksheet: Write a postcard

Imagine you are a first-class passenger on-board the Titanic. Write a postcard to a friend about what life is like on-board the ship.

Copyright © Clare Horrie and Rachel Hillman, 2020

Titanic: What happened?

⟳ Lesson overview

Lesson enquiry question

What happened the night the Titanic sank?

Resources required

Sources:

❶ Iceberg field.

❷ Jack Phillips, Marconi Operator.

❸ Lifeboat.

❹ Sand memorial.

Other:

- Question sheet: What happened the night the Titanic sank? Photocopy one per pair.
- Worksheet: What happened on 14th April 1912? Photocopy one per pupil.

Lesson focus

Describe:

Two or three facts about the Titanic and what happened to it.

Explain:

Explain some of the events that took place on the night of 14th April 1912.

Curriculum link:

Significant historical events, people and places in pupils' own locality.

❶ Iceberg field.

❷ Jack Phillips, Marconi Operator.

❸ Lifeboat.

❹ Sand memorial.

🚀 Starter activity

Recap with the pupils what they have learnt about the Titanic from the previous lesson. Explain that in this lesson they are going to find out more about what happened to the Titanic on 14th April 1912, the date it sank.

Show the image of the iceberg field on the whiteboard. Before offering any further information, ask the pupils questions about the image:

- What can you see?
- What do you think the large shapes in the background of the image are?
- What do you think this has to do with the Titanic?

Now explain that this is a photograph of the ice-field (icebergs) that the Titanic hit and ask the pupils:

- What are your impressions of the ice-field?
- Do you think that the icebergs look big enough to have caused so much damage to such a huge ship?

Explain that icebergs are even bigger underneath the water, and that these icebergs were about 30 metres tall (the height of six double-decker buses stacked on top of each other!).

✏️ Creative activity

Pupils could create simple storyboards showing some of the different events that occurred on 14th April 1912. For example:

1) the iceberg sighting

2) Titanic hitting the iceberg

3) Jack Phillips sending out emergency telegrams

4) passengers being evacuated into lifeboats.

You can photocopy and hand out the worksheet on page 34 to support this activity.

⭐ Main activity

Explain that in this lesson pupils are going to find out more about the Titanic and the things that happened the night it sank.

Split the class into pairs and hand each pair a copy of the photographs of Jack Phillips, the lifeboat and the sand memorial, as well as a copy of the question sheet on page 33. Ask the pupils to investigate each photograph to find out what it tells us about the events of 14th April 1912 and what happened to the Titanic. Tell them to use the questions on the sheet as prompts.

Once the pupils have had an opportunity to look at the different sources, bring them back together to feed back as a class. What did they find interesting? Why? Now talk to the pupils about the additional information about each source below, and how this can help us to understand more about the Titanic and what happened to it.

Photograph of Jack Phillips

This is a photograph of Jack Phillips. Jack was the senior radio officer, responsible for sending out signals for help until the moment the Titanic sank.

Photograph of lifeboat

This is a photograph of one of the lifeboats that passengers on-board the Titanic used to escape. There were not enough lifeboats for all of the people on-board and many of the lifeboats left the ship before they had been completely filled to capacity.

Photograph of sand memorial

This is a photograph of a memorial made out of sand on Bournemouth beach. It was made by people there as a temporary shrine and a way to remember those who had died in the disaster.

Copyright © Clare Horrie and Rachel Hillman, 2020

📝 Question sheet: What happened the night the Titanic sank?

Look at the three photographs. What do they tell us about what happened when the Titanic sank?

Photograph of Jack Phillips

1. What can you see?

2. How is this man dressed?

3. Do you think he was a passenger or a crew member on-board the Titanic?

Photograph of lifeboat

1. What can you see?

2. What do you think these people are doing?

Photograph of sand memorial on Bournemouth beach

1. What can you see?

2. Why do you think this sand model was made?

✏️ Worksheet: What happened on 14th April 1912?

Create a storyboard showing the events of 14th April 1912, the night the Titanic sank. Draw a picture and write a description for each event.

Copyright © Clare Horrie and Rachel Hillman, 2020

Titanic: What were the lessons learned?

⊙ Lesson overview

Lesson enquiry question

What were the lessons learned from the sinking of the Titanic?

Resources required

Sources:

1 Cover page of Court of Enquiry into RMS Titanic.

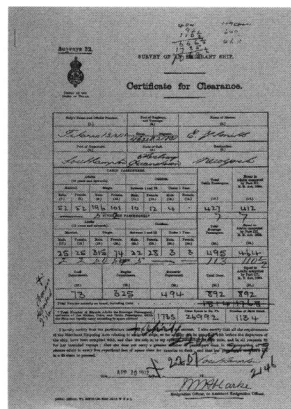

2 Document about lifeboats.

3 Photograph of lifeboat.

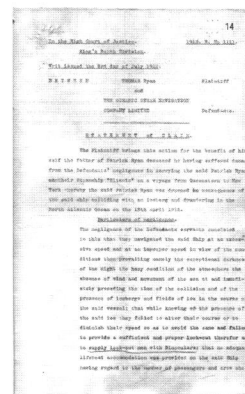

4 Document suing Oceanic Steam Navigation Co. Ltd.

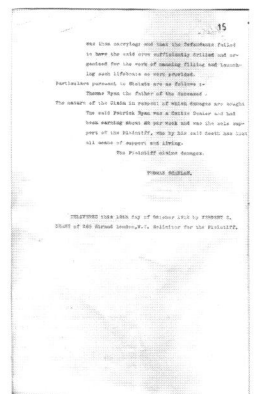

Other:

- Simplified transcripts for sources 1 and 4.
- Question sheet: What caused the Titanic to sink? Photocopy one per pair.

Lesson focus

Describe:

Describe what happened to the Titanic.

Explain:

Explain one of the lessons learned from the disaster.

Curriculum link:

Significant historical events, people and places in pupils' own locality.

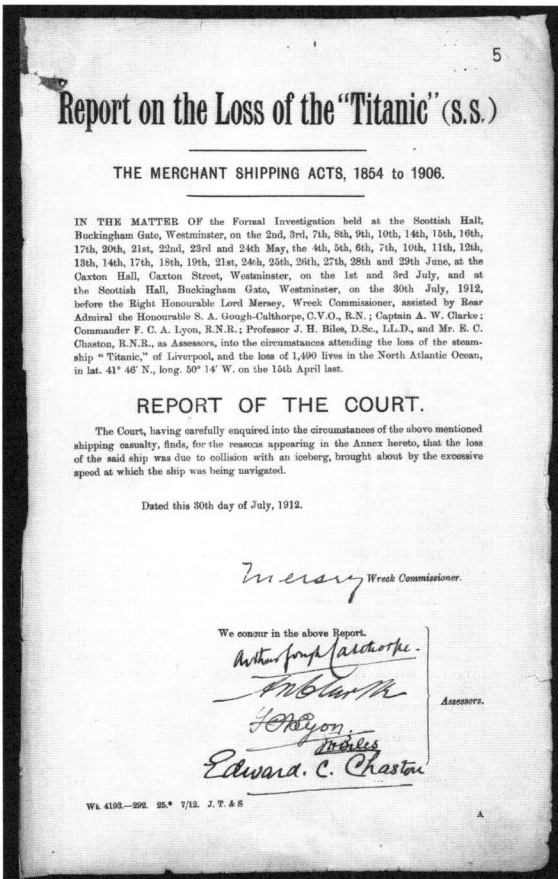

1 Cover page of Court of Enquiry into RMS Titanic.

2 Document about lifeboats.

3 Photograph of lifeboat.

4 Document suing Oceanic Steam Navigation Co. Ltd.

🚀 Starter activity

Explain that after the Titanic sank, the government launched a big enquiry into what happened and what had gone wrong. As part of this enquiry they spoke to survivors of the disaster, as well as crew from other ships who had picked up the Titanic's emergency messages.

Show the cover page of the Court of Enquiry into RMS Titanic on the whiteboard. Ask the pupils questions about the image:

- Can you spot any important names? (They should be able to spot 'Titanic'.)
- What do you think the title means? What is it telling us about the Titanic?
- Can you find a date?

Explain that this is the cover page of the enormous investigation that was held into the disaster and gives the main reason why it was believed the Titanic sank. Read the simplified transcript for the cover page aloud to the class. Can the pupils explain what the enquiry thought caused the Titanic to hit the iceberg?

✏️ Creative activity

Pupils could design a poster for a film all about the Titanic. Explain that their posters have to include three pieces of information that they've learnt about the Titanic from the different sources in each of the three lessons about the disaster. For example, they could choose to show:

1. the luxury of the ship
2. the loss of the binoculars, which meant the look-out didn't see the iceberg soon enough
3. the emergency telegrams that were sent as the ship was sinking.

⭐ Main activity

Explain that in this lesson pupils are going to find out some of the lessons that were learnt from the Titanic, and how these have been used to make things safe for people travelling by sea today.

Split the class into pairs and hand each pair a copy of the document about lifeboats, lifebelts and lifebuoys, the photograph of the lifeboat, and the document suing Oceanic Steam Navigation Co. Ltd, as well as a copy of the question sheet on page 39. You can also provide the pupils with the simplified transcript of the final document if necessary, available on page 38. In pairs, using the questions as prompts, ask the pupils to investigate each document to find out what it tells us about the things that went wrong and caused the Titanic to sink.

Once the pupils have had an opportunity to look at the different sources, bring them back together to feed back as a class. What mistakes were made that caused the Titanic to sink? What lessons do they think were learnt from the disaster? As part of the discussion, you can share with them the following information about each source.

Document about lifeboats, lifebelts and lifebuoys

Explain that there were 2,224 passengers on-board. There were not enough lifeboats or lifebelts for each person. Following the disaster, ships had to ensure that they had enough lifeboats and life jackets for everyone on-board.

Photograph of lifeboat

Explain that because the crew hadn't been properly trained to use the lifeboats, they hadn't made sure that each lifeboat was full up before releasing it from the Titanic. This wasted a lot of space and meant that more people died. Today there are proper training drills for the crews and passengers.

Document suing Oceanic Steam Navigation Co. Ltd

Explain that this document is accusing the Oceanic Steam Navigation Co. Ltd (who owned the White Star Line and the Titanic) of making lots of mistakes. It is believed that the look-out men had no binoculars, which made it almost impossible for them to spot the iceberg until it was too late.

Copyright © Clare Horrie and Rachel Hillman, 2020

☰ Simplified transcript

Cover page of Court of Enquiry into RMS Titanic

Report on the Loss of 'Titanic' (SS) The Merchant Shipping Acts 1854–1906

———————

In the matter of the formal investigation held into the loss of Titanic and the deaths of 1,490 people in the North Atlantic Ocean on the 15th April 1912.

Report of the Court

The court, having carefully looked at the matter, find that the loss of Titanic was due to the collision with an iceberg, brought about by the excessive [too fast] speed that the ship was travelling.

———————

Dated 30th July 1912
Signed by Wreck Commissioner
Signed by Assessors

🗐 Simplified transcript

Document suing Oceanic Steam Navigation Co. Ltd

Suing the owners; the statement of Claim and Verdict in the case of Ryan v. the Oceanic Steam Navigation Co. Ltd, 3 June 1912.

In the High Court of Justice. 1912. R.
No. 1111.
King's Bench Division.
Writ issued the 3rd day of July 1912.

BETWEEN THOMAS Ryan Plaintiff [person who is bringing the case to court]
and
THE OCEANIC STEAM NAVIGATION
COMPANY LIMITED Defendants

STATEMENT OF CLAIM.
The Plaintiff brings this case as the father of Patrick Ryan who died on-board Titanic on 15th April 1912.

The Defendants sailed Titanic speeds that were too fast for the dark conditions of night, and the calmness of the sea (which made the icebergs harder to spot). The Defendants knew that there were icebergs on the route that they'd taken, and they did not slow their speed, change their course or provide the look-out men with binoculars. There were also not enough lifeboats to give each passenger and crew member a place. The Defendants did not make sure that the crew had practised enough to fill the lifeboats properly in the event of an emergency.

Copyright © Clare Horrie and Rachel Hillman, 2020

📝 Question sheet: What caused the Titanic to sink?

Look at the three sources. What do they tell us about what went wrong and caused the Titanic to sink?

Document about lifeboats, lifebelts and lifebuoys

1. How many people could all of the lifeboats hold? Were there enough places in the boats to carry everyone on-board?

2. How many lifebelts and lifebuoys were there?

Photograph of lifeboat

1. What can you see?

Document suing Oceanic Steam Navigation Co. Ltd

1. What do you think a look-out man is?

2. Why didn't the look-out man spot the iceberg in time?

Florence Nightingale

⊙ Lesson overview

Lesson enquiry question

Why do we remember Florence Nightingale?

Resources required

Sources:

1 Florence Nightingale's birth certificate.

2 Photograph of Florence Nightingale.

3 Extract from the 'Report upon the state of the hospitals of the British army in the Crimea and Scutari', February 1855.

4 Florence Nightingale's Crimean War carriage.

Other:

- Transcripts for sources 1 and 3.
- Simplified transcript and glossary for source 3.

Lesson focus

Describe:

Describe details of Florence Nightingale's life and her achievement, using an original extract from a report on the state of the hospitals of the British army in the Crimea.

Explain:

Explain that Florence Nightingale (1820–1910) worked as a nurse during the Crimean War (1854–1856). She was also a statistician and social reformer. She was responsible for turning nursing into a highly skilled and respected profession.

Curriculum link:

The lives of significant individuals.

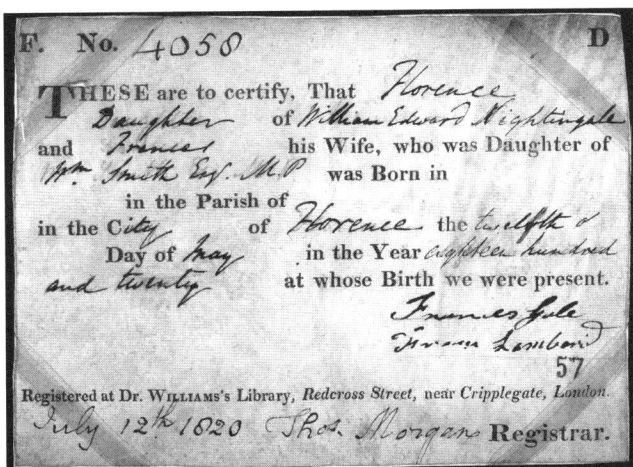

1 Florence Nightingale's birth certificate.

2 Photograph of Florence Nightingale.

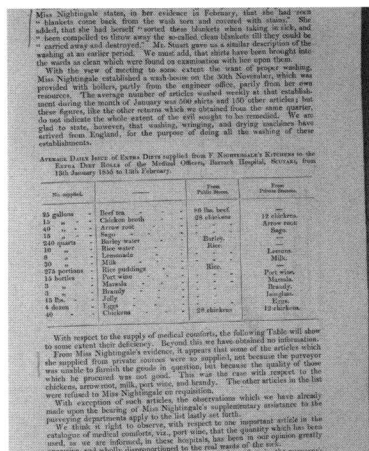

3 Extract from the 'Report upon the state of the hospitals of the British army in the Crimea and Scutari', February 1855.

4 Florence Nightingale's Crimean War carriage.

 Copyright © Clare Horrie and Rachel Hillman, 2020

🚀 Starter activity

Reveal the first source (Florence Nightingale's birth certificate) as a mystery document to get pupils thinking. Use the transcript if necessary. Once the pupils have offered some initial observations, take a look at the second source (photograph of Florence Nightingale) together. You can either print these sources out or project them on a whiteboard. Discuss the following questions with the pupils:

- When was Florence Nightingale born?
- Where was she born?
- What did her grandfather do?
- What was her mother's name?
- What was her father's name?
- When was her birth registered in London? Why was this later?
- Why do you think she was called Florence?
- What can you tell from the photograph about Florence Nightingale? (Think about her dress, expression and social background.)
- Do you think it was unusual for her to want to be a nurse at that time? Can you explain why?

⭐ Main activity

Print out copies of the third source (the report extract) or project it on a whiteboard. You can refer to or hand out the transcript or simplified version if you wish. Highlight and define any difficult words and read the source with the pupils. Ensure they understand the content and discuss the following questions as you read each section:

Paragraph 1:

- What did Florence think about the state of the blankets after they had been washed?
- What did she do with them?
- What was wrong with the shirts that were supposed to be clean?

Paragraph 2:

- How did Florence Nightingale try to solve the problem of dirty clothes and bedding?
- What else was done to help the problem of keeping things clean?

Diet table (content):

This table lists extra items of food and drink provided by Florence Nightingale's hospital kitchen. Look through the table together, using the glossary to help. Discuss the last columns. One shows the goods provided by the army hospital stores and the other shows the goods supplied privately by Florence Nightingale. This means she must have raised money privately to pay for these things.

- Are you surprised by anything that the soldiers were eating and drinking?
- Would people in hospital eat and drink these things today?
- Can you give reasons for your answers?

Final paragraphs below table:

- Why did Florence Nightingale still supply goods that the army stores already had?
- What item did the government think was not necessary for the soldiers to have in hospital? Why do you think they thought this?
- What other information does the report provide? (It gives details on diets, so we know how the sick were cared for and treatments they received. The report also describes the lack of cleanliness in the hospitals and shows the numbers admitted.)
- Can we trust it more than another type of source, for example a painting of a hospital?
- What conclusions can we come to about Florence Nightingale's work from this report? (She was highly organised, kept records, raised money to buy things that soldiers needed and was taken seriously by the government.)
- What conclusions can we have about her character? (She must have been a very strong-minded woman, as somebody from her class was expected to marry and not work.)
- Why was her work significant? (It improved survival rates in hospitals; the role of nurses changed; it altered attitudes to women.)

✏️ Creative activity

Pupils write a museum label for the fourth source: Florence Nightingale's carriage used in the Crimea to transport the wounded to hospital. They should explain in their label why we remember her.

Transcript

Florence Nightingale's birth certificate

F. No 4058   D

THESE are to certify, **That** Florence

Daughter of William Edward Nightingale

and Frances his Wife, who was Daughter of [William] Smith Esq. M.P. was Born in

in the Parish of

in the City of Florence **the** twelfth

Day of May **in the Year** eighteen hundred and twenty

at whose Birth we were present:

Frances Gale

Francesca Lambert

57

Registered at Dr WILLIAMS'S Library, Redcross Street, near Cripplegate, London.

July 12th 1820 [Thomas] Morgan **Registrar.**

Copyright © Clare Horrie and Rachel Hillman, 2020

📄 Transcript

Extract from the 'Report upon the state of the hospitals of the British army in the Crimea and Scutari', February 1855

Miss Nightingale states in her evidence in February, that she had seen "blankets come back from the wash torn and covered in stains." She added, that she had herself "sorted these blankets when taking in sick, and added "been compelled to throw away the so-called clean blankets till they could be "carried away and destroyed". Mr. Stuart gave us a similar description of the washing at an earlier period. We must add, that shirts have been brought into the ward as clean which were found on examination with lice upon them.

With the view of meeting to some extent the want of proper washing, Miss Nightingale established a wash-house on the 30th November, which was provided with boilers, partly from the engineer office, partly from her own resources. The average number of articles washed weekly at the establishment during the month of January was 500 shirts and 150 other articles; but these figures, like the other returns which we returned from the same quarter, do not indicate the whole extent of the evil sought be remedied. We are glad to state, however, that washing, wringing, and drying machines have arrived from England, for the purpose of doing all the washing of these establishments.

AVERAGE DAILY ISSUE OF EXTRA DIETS supplied from F. NIGHTINGALE'S KITCHENS to the EXTRA DIET ROLLS of the Medical Officers, Barrack Hospital, SCUTARI, from 13th January 1855 to 13th February.

No. supplied	-----------------------	From Public Stores	From Private Sources
25 Gallons	Beef tea	80lbs. beef	-
15 "	Chicken broth	28 chickens	12 chickens
40 "	Arrow root	----------------	Arrow root
15 "	Sago	----------------	Sago
240 quarts	Barley Water	Barley	-------
10 "	Rice water	Rice	-------
8 "	Lemonade	-----------------	Lemons
30 "	Milk	------------------	Milk
275 portions	Rice puddings	Rice	-------
15 bottles	Port wine	------------------	Port wine
3 "	Marsala	------------------	Marsala
3 "	Brandy	------------------	Brandy
15lbs	Jelly	------------------	Isinglass
4 dozen	Eggs	------------------	Eggs
40	Chickens	28 chickens	12 chickens

From Miss Nightingale's evidence, it appears that some of the articles which she supplied from private sources were so supplied, not because the purveyor was unable to furnish the goods in question, but because the quality of those which he procured was not good. This was the case with respect to the chickens, arrow root, milk, port wine, and brandy. The other articles in the list were refused to Miss Nightingale on requisition.

With exception of such articles, the observations which we have already made upon the bearing of Miss Nightingale's supplementary assistance to the purveying departments apply to the list lastly set forth.

We think it right to observe, with respect to one important article in the catalogue of medical comforts, viz., port wine, that the quantity which has been used, as we are informed, in these hospitals, has been in our opinion greatly excessive, and wholly disproportioned to the real wants of the sick.

Copyright © Clare Horrie and Rachel Hillman, 2020

☰ Simplified transcript

Extract from the 'Report upon the state of the hospitals of the British army in the Crimea and Scutari', February 1855

Miss Nightingale said she had seen "blankets come back from the wash torn and covered in stains." She had to throw away so-called clean blankets. Also, shirts which were supposed to be clean came into the hospital covered in lice.

To improve washing in the hospital, Miss Nightingale set up a wash-house with boilers, [to heat water] paid for by the engineer's office and her own money. In January, 500 shirts and 150 other things were washed; but these numbers do not show how bad the washing problem was. However, washing, wringing, and drying machines have arrived from England, to do the washing here.

From Miss Nightingale's evidence, she supplied some of the things that were needed. This was because the quality of things from the hospital suppliers was not good, rather than a shortage of goods. This was the case with respect to the chickens, arrow root, milk, port wine, and brandy. The other articles in the list were refused to Miss Nightingale when she asked for them.

We would like to point out that the amount of port wine used in these hospitals is too much and not necessary for the sick.

Copyright © Clare Horrie and Rachel Hillman, 2020

Glossary

Glossary of terms

Arrow root: a starchy powder possibly used to draw out poison from wounds

Sago: starch used to make puddings, a bit like semolina

Rice water: rice soaked in water, said to be used to stop diarrhoea and upset stomach

Barley water: a drink made from boiling up barley and flavoured, used to build up a patient's strength

Beef tea: drink made from boiling pieces of beef, used to build up patient's strength

Marsala: type of wine

Brandy: very strong alcoholic drink

Port: strong, sweet type of red wine drunk at end of meal

Isinglass: a form of gelatine made from fish innards used to make jelly or glue

Weights and measures:

Gallon: 4.5 litres approximately

Quarts: one quarter of a gallon, roughly just over a litre

1lb: 454 grams

1 ounce: 28 grams

16 ounces: 1lb

Copyright © Clare Horrie and Rachel Hillman, 2020

Elizabeth I

⟳ Lesson overview

Lesson enquiry question

What can the documents reveal about Elizabeth I?

Resources required

Sources:

1 Great Seal of Elizabeth I.

2 Plea roll from Elizabeth I's reign.

Other:

• Worksheet: Design your own seal. Photocopy one per pupil.

Lesson focus

Describe:

Who was Elizabeth I?

Explain:

Explain what the documents can tell us about Elizabeth I and the way in which she wanted to be perceived and portrayed.

Curriculum link:

The lives of individuals who have contributed to national and international achievements.

1 Great Seal of Elizabeth I.

2 Plea roll from Elizabeth I's reign.

Copyright © Clare Horrie and Rachel Hillman, 2020

🚀 Starter activity

Reveal the image of Elizabeth I's Great Seal as a mystery document. Print enough copies of the Seal for one between two, and ask the pupils to spend five minutes with a partner highlighting all of the different things that they can spot in the image. Encourage them to annotate the document and to label some of things that they have noticed.

Bring the pupils back together and ask them about the things that they have spotted. You could annotate a large image of the seal projected on the whiteboard as they feed back their answers. Use the following questions as prompts:

- What have you highlighted? What do you think these things are?
- What have you found interesting?
- Do you think that this person is important? Why or why not?
- What type of document do you think this is? What do you think it might have been used for?

Explain that this person is very important and that she was a queen called Elizabeth I, who reigned from 1558 to 1603. Many historians have described her as a strong queen with a very successful reign.

Return to the image of the seal and the things that the pupils highlighted. Ask the pupils how these pictures and images tell us that Elizabeth I was a successful and great queen. Draw your pupils' attention to the following images if they haven't spotted them already:

- Can you see the hands emerging from the clouds holding Elizabeth's cape away from her body? What might this suggest? (She has the support of God and has been chosen to rule. This is called 'divine right'.)
- Can you spot the Tudor rose? What does this tell us? (Elizabeth is descended from the Tudor dynasty, the family that brought peace to England after the War of the Roses.)
- Can you spot the harp and the fleur-de-lys? What do these tell us? (The harp is a symbol of Ireland and the fleur-de-lys is a symbol of the French monarchy. Elizabeth is using these to show her claim and right to rule over both Ireland and parts of France.)

You could also look at the way Elizabeth is dressed in this image. Ask the pupils:

- How is Elizabeth dressed? Look at her hairstyle, her dress and her ruff. What do these tell us about her importance and wealth? (She is well dressed and fashionable, reflecting her status and significance.)
- What objects is Elizabeth holding? What meaning do these have? (She is holding the orb and sceptre, both of which are symbols of monarchy and rule.)

- Can the pupils spot the writing at the bottom of the seal? This is written in Latin, but in English it means 'Elizabeth, by grace of God, Queen of England, France and Ireland, Defender of the Faith'. (This again demonstrates her right to rule and her role as Head of the Church of England.)

You should now explain to pupils that this document is a seal and was a way of 'signing' and authenticating official documents. It was also a form of propaganda, allowing Elizabeth to show the attributes and qualities that she wanted people to associate with her rule.

⭐ Main activity

Explain Elizabeth's rule in more detail. You could mention that she descended from the Tudor monarchy and her parents were King Henry VIII and Anne Boleyn. Elizabeth I had many challenges during her reign: the issue of religion, the threat of foreign invasion and widespread poverty. At a time when women were not seen as strong enough to rule without the support of a husband, Elizabeth faced much opposition from those who thought she should marry, but she never married and stayed single until she died in 1603.

Explain to the pupils that, as a woman ruling alone, it was even more important for Elizabeth to portray an image of strength and power. One way she achieved this was through the use of her image. Give each pupil a copy of the image of Elizabeth's plea roll. Ask them to work in pairs, thinking about the questions below:

- What can you see in the image?
- Why do you think Elizabeth has chosen to show herself in this way?
- What words would you use to describe Elizabeth in this picture?

Bring the pupils back together and ask them to feed back their findings. Ask the pupils:

- Do you think that this image shows Elizabeth as a strong queen, in command of her country? Why or why not?
- Which document (the seal or the plea roll) do they think is better at portraying Elizabeth as a powerful queen? Why do they think this?

✏️ Creative activity

Ask the pupils to design their own seals. What would they choose to show if they wanted to tell others about themselves in this way? They could choose their favourite food or hobbies, or perhaps their best qualities, such as kindness or humour. Photocopy the worksheet on page 48 to help support this activity.

Copyright © Clare Horrie and Rachel Hillman, 2020

📝 Worksheet: Design your own seal

Design your own seal to tell people about yourself. You can show your hobbies, your favourite food or your personality.

What have you chosen to include on your seal and why?

_____

_____

_____

_____

_____

_____

_____

Copyright © Clare Horrie and Rachel Hillman, 2020

Walter Tull

⊙ Lesson overview

Lesson enquiry question

Why was Walter Tull important?

Resources required

Sources:

1 Football team picture, Tottenham Hotspur FC. 1909.

2 Walter Tull's application for a temporary commission in the army.

Other:

- Transcript for source 2.
- Walter Tull timeline. Photocopy one per pair.

Lesson focus

Describe:

Describe why Walter Tull is considered a significant person in history using two documents.

Explain:

Explain that Walter Tull (1888–1918) was of dual heritage; his mother was white British and his father was African-Caribbean. Tull was a talented footballer and played as an amateur and professional before the First World War. He was commissioned as an officer in 1917 at a time when the army required officers to be of 'pure European descent'. For his army service he was recommended a Military Cross.

Curriculum link:

The lives of significant individuals.

1 Football team picture, Tottenham Hotspur FC. 1909.

🚀 Starter activity

Show the pupils the football team picture of Tottenham Hotspur in 1909 and point out Walter Tull in the front row. Ask the pupils:

- What can you see?
- How do you know it's a team?

What's in the background? Tell the pupils a little more about Walter Tull, using the information on the timeline on page 52 to help.

❷ Walter Tull's application for a temporary commission in the army.

⭐ Main activity

Introduce the second source: Walter Tull's application for a temporary commission in the army. Point to the title of the document and the phrase 'temporary commission'. This was a temporary promotion as an officer who could then lead men on the battlefield. Explain that as the First World War progressed, more men were needed to fight, and therefore more men were needed to take up the senior positions in the army. This enabled men from a wider variety of social backgrounds to become officers. Walter Tull was made an officer, even though black soldiers were not supposed to become officers in the British Army at this time.

Ask the pupils to look carefully at the second source and think about the following questions in pairs or small groups. Hand each pair or group a printed copy of the source and the transcript if needed.

- What was Walter Tull's full name?
- When was he born?
- Was he married?
- What type of job do you think Walter had when this document was made? Why do you think this?
- Why do both documents you have looked at reveal the significance of Walter Tull in history?

Once the pupils have discussed these questions in their pairs or groups, ask them to feed back to the whole class and facilitate a more detailed discussion about why Walter Tull was important. Make sure the discussion covers the following information:

- Walter Tull was important because he was one of the first black officers in the British Army, which paved the way for equal opportunities for others. At the time, only white, British-born men could be trained as officers.
- He was a very brave soldier and leader of men. He fought at the Battle of the Somme, at Messines and at Passchendaele.
- He was one of the very first black footballers to play in the First Division, which was significant in making the sport start to be more inclusive.

✏️ Creative activity

Working in pairs, pupils interview Walter Tull about his life. They take it in turns to play both Walter and the interviewer. You can provide them with the timeline on page 52 or relevant topic books to support them.

Copyright © Clare Horrie and Rachel Hillman, 2020

📄 Transcript

Walter Tull's application for a temporary commission in the army

Walter Tull (1888–1918) was of dual heritage; his mother was white British and his father was African-Caribbean. Tull was commissioned* as an officer in 1917 at a time when the army required officers to be of 'pure European descent'. This was an important challenge to a racist policy. For his army service he was recommended a Military Cross. This is his application for a temporary commission form in 1917.

*A commissioned officer commands a military unit.

1.	Name in full (Surname, Christian names)	Tull, Walter Daniel
2.	Date of birth	April 28th 1888
3.	Whether married	No
4.	Whether of pure European descent	No
5.	Whether a British subject by birth or naturalization. (State which, and if by naturalization attach a certificate from the Home Office)	By Birth
6.	Nationality by birth of father (if naturalized, state date)	West Indian
7.	Permanent address	419, St. Vincent Street, Glasgow
8.	Present address for correspondence	23rd Battalion Middlesex Regiment, "C" Company, B.E.F. [British Expeditionary Force]
9.	Whether now serving, or previously served, in any other Government Department (Home, Indian, or Colonial). If so give particulars.	Now serving. 21 months in 17th Battalion Middlesex Regiment 2 months in 23rd Battalion [Middlesex Regiment]
10.	Whether able to ride	No.
11.	Whether now serving, or previously served, in any branch of His Majesty's Naval or Military Forces, or in the Officers Training Corps. If so state:-	
	(a). Regiment, Corps, or Contingent	17th Battalion, Middlesex Regiment
	(b). Date of appointment	December 21st 1914
	(c). Rank	Sergeant
	(d). Date of retirement, resignation or discharge	
	(e). Circumstances of retirement, resignation or discharge	
	Whether an application for a commission has been previously made, if so, on what date and for what branch of the service.	Nil

📝 Worksheet: Walter Tull timeline

28th April 1888: Walter was born in Folkestone, Kent. His father was from Barbados and his mother was from Kent. Walter's parents died when he was nine years old. Walter and his brother were brought up in an orphanage in Bethnal Green, East London.

1908: Walter got involved in football and was signed by Clapham FC.

1909: Walter was signed by Tottenham Hotspur FC. He was the second person of Afro-Caribbean mixed heritage to play in the top division of the Football League.

1911: Walter Tull moved to Northampton Town FC where he played half-back.

1914: At the start of the First World War, Walter joined the 17th (1st Football) Battalion of the Middlesex Regiment as a lance corporal.

1915: Walter served in France. Later, he was placed in hospital for shell shock.

1916: Walter returned to action in September and fought in the Battle of the Somme. Walter returned to Britain for officer training and rejoined the 23rd Battalion of the Middlesex Regiment as a second lieutenant.

1917: Despite army rules that forbade a 'person of colour' being commissioned as an officer (a leader of men), Walter was promoted to lieutenant after officer training school at Gailes, Scotland. Tull was the first Afro-Caribbean/mixed-heritage man to be commissioned as an infantry officer in the British Army.

1918: Walter died aged 29 whilst leading an attack on the Western Front during the second Battle of the Somme in March. The Commanding Officer of the 23rd Battalion recommended him for a Military Cross for bravery.

Copyright © Clare Horrie and Rachel Hillman, 2020

Noor Khan

⊙ Lesson overview

Lesson enquiry question

What can four documents reveal about Noor Khan?

Resources required

Four sources from Noor Khan's file:

1 Training report 2.

2 Photograph of Noor Khan.

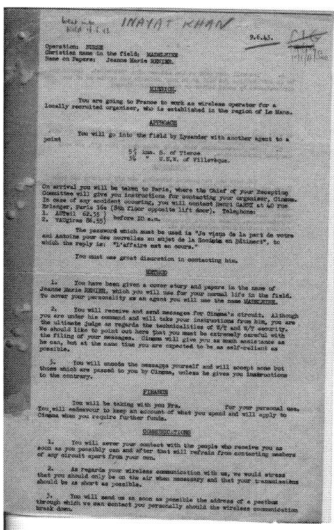

3 Mission instructions.

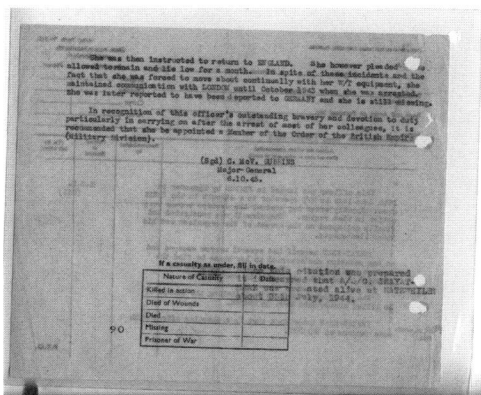

4 Major General Gubbins' report.

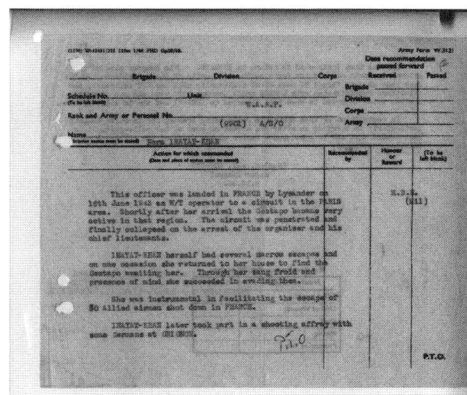

Other:

· Simplified transcripts for sources 3 and 4.
· Highlighters.
· Question sheet: Finding out more about Noor Khan.
  Photocopy one per pair or group.

Lesson focus

Describe:

Describe who Noor Khan was.

Explain:

Explain what the documents can tell us about Noor Khan and the role she played during the Second World War.

Curriculum link:

The lives of individuals who have contributed to national and international achievements.

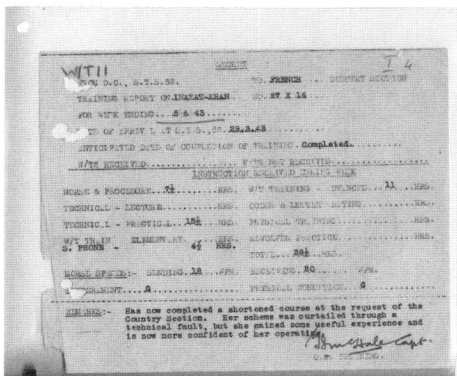

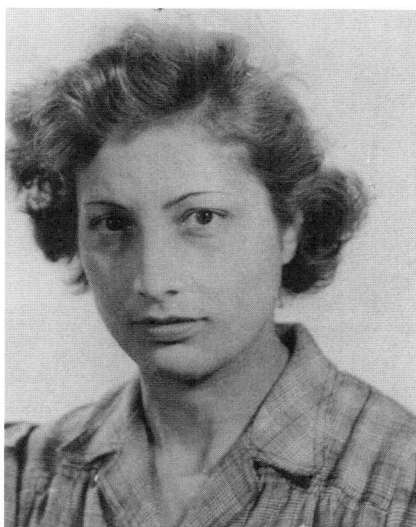

1 Training report 2.

2 Photograph of Noor Khan.

3 Mission instructions.

4 Major General Gubbins' report.

🚀 Starter activity

Reveal the training report (source 1) as a mystery document and ask the pupils to spend two minutes with a partner, chatting about their first impressions of the document. Make sure each pair has a printed copy of the document. Use the following questions as prompts if required:

- What does the document look like?
- How has it been made? Is it handwritten?
- Do you have any ideas about what type of document this is? Is it a letter, a list or something else?

Now ask the pupils to feed back to the rest of the class. Accept all answers as plausible at this stage. Give the pupils two further minutes in their pairs and ask them to highlight anything they find interesting on the document. This might be words, numbers or annotations.

Bring the pupils back together and ask them about the things that they have spotted. You could annotate a large image of the document projected on the whiteboard as they feed back their answers. Ask the pupils why they highlighted these things. Have they any further ideas about what the document could be?

Explain that this document is a report. Talk about how the children have school reports at the end of each school year. Do they think this is somebody's school report? Why or why not?

Explain that it is a report of a person called Noor Khan (highlight her name at the top of the document). Noor Khan was training to do a very important job during the Second World War. She was training to be a spy! This document is one of her training reports and it tells us how well she was doing at spy school. At this point, if the pupils haven't already made reference to this, draw their attention to some of the things that Noor Khan was learning about, for example:

- W/T training (wireless operator training, in order to transmit and receive secret messages)
- revolver practice (using a gun)
- codes and letter writing (sending information in code)
- physical training (sporting activity to keep fit).

Ask the pupils why Noor Khan might need to learn some of these things to be a spy.

Show pupils the photograph of Noor Khan (source 2). Explain that this is taken from her spy file. At this point you could tell the pupils a little bit about Noor Khan's background and how she came to join the SOE (Special Operations Executive).

⭐ Main activity

Explain that pupils are now going to find out more about Noor Khan and her job as a spy. Tell them that they will have two further documents to look at and some questions to help them. What can they find out about Noor Khan from these documents? The pupils can work in pairs or small groups. Hand out printed copies of each source and a copy of the question sheet on page 57. You can also give the pupils the simplified transcripts of each source if needed, but ask them to have a go at reading the original documents initially.

Mission instructions:

1. What type of document do you think this is? Why do you think this?
2. What instructions has Noor Khan been given?
3. What code name has she been given? Why does she now need to use this name?

Major General Gubbins' report:

1. What happened shortly after Noor Khan arrived in France?
2. What did Noor Khan bravely manage to do?
3. What is Major General Gubbins' opinion of Noor Khan? How do you know this?
4. What has Noor Khan been awarded?

Bring the pupils back together and ask them to feed back their findings. What have they found out about Noor Khan?

Explain that in October 1943, two years before the end of the war, Noor Khan was arrested by the Gestapo (the German secret police). In November she was sent to Pforzheim Prison in Germany, where she refused to give away any information about the Allies. The following year, in September 1944, Noor Khan was transferred to Dachau concentration camp where she was executed. For her courage during the war, Noor Khan was posthumously awarded the George Cross in 1949.

🕹 Creative activity

Pupils could investigate the special training programme that was used at SOE training schools. The National Archives website has some excellent materials about their training available at www.nationalarchives.gov.uk/education/homefront/spies and www.nationalarchives.gov.uk/education/worldwar2/index-of-resources/western-europe/resistance. Pupils could then create their own mini spy handbooks or posters as aide-memoires for would-be spies.

 Copyright © Clare Horrie and Rachel Hillman, 2020

☰ Simplified transcript

Mission instructions

<u>INAYAT KHAN</u>

Went into

field [enemy territory] 16.6.43

Operation [name of spy mission]: NURSE

Christian name in the field: MADELEINE

Name on papers [official documents]: Jeanne Marie RENIER

<u>Mission</u>

You are going to France to work as a wireless operator [receiving and sending messages to/from England]. You will work for a spy network located in Le Mans [an area of France].

<u>Approach</u>

You will arrive in France with another spy on a Lysander aeroplane at a specific location.

When you arrive, you will be taken to Paris. Here you will be given instructions on how to contact the organiser of your spy network, code-named CINEMA.

There is a password you must use.

You must be very careful when you contact him.

<u>METHOD</u>

1. You will take the name of Jeanne Marie RENIER. When working as an agent you will use the name MADELEINE.

2. You will receive and send messages for Cinema's spy network [Cinema is the person in charge of this network]. You will take instruction from him and he will tell you what to do.

3. You will only take messages given to you by Cinema. You will put them into code yourself.

Copyright © Clare Horrie and Rachel Hillman, 2020

☰ Simplified transcript

Major General Gubbins' report

Unit: WAAF [Women's Auxiliary Air Force]

Name: Nora Inayat Khan ['Nora' is sometimes used instead of 'Noor']

Action for which commended [awarded recognition or praise]

This officer [Noor Khan] landed in France on 16th June 1943 as a Wireless Operator [sending and receiving wireless messages to/from England]. Shortly after she arrived, the Gestapo [secret German police] arrested the main organiser of her spy network and many of the other spies.

Noor herself had a few narrow escapes. On one occasion she had come back to her house to find the Gestapo waiting for her. Remaining calm, she managed to escape them.

She helped the escape of 30 Allied airmen who had been shot down in France.

She was told to return to ENGLAND. But she asked to stay in France and carry on with her work even though it was very dangerous. She lost contact with London in October 1943 when she was arrested by the Nazis.

In recognition of her bravery and commitment to carry on with her work (even after the arrest of other spies in her network), it is recommended that she be appointed a Member of the Order of the British Empire [MBE – this is awarded for excellent service to the country].

Major General Gubbins
6.10.45

Copyright © Clare Horrie and Rachel Hillman, 2020

✍ Question sheet: Finding out more about Noor Khan

Look at the two sources: the mission instructions and Major General Gubbins' report. What can you find out about Noor Khan from these documents? Answer these questions to help.

Mission instructions

1. What type of document do you think this is? Why do you think this?

_____

_____

2. What instructions has Noor Khan been given?

_____

_____

3. What code name has she been given? Why does she now need to use this name?

_____

_____

Major General Gubbins' report

1. What happened shortly after Noor Khan arrived in France?

_____

_____

2. What did Noor Khan bravely manage to do?

_____

_____

3. What is Major General Gubbins' opinion of Noor Khan? How do you know this?

_____

_____

4. What has Noor Khan been awarded?

_____

_____

Copyright © Clare Horrie and Rachel Hillman, 2020

Edith Cavell

⟳ Lesson overview

Lesson enquiry question

Why do we remember Edith Cavell?

Resources required

Sources:

1 Drawing called 'Faith and courage in death, an allegory of Edith Cavell' from the *Illustrated London News*.

2 Statement issued from Foreign Office commenting on the execution of Edith Cavell.

Other:

• Transcript for source 2.

Lesson focus

Describe:

Describe what Edith Cavell did in the First World War.

Explain:

Explain that Edith Cavell (1865–1915) worked as a nurse in Belgium whilst it was occupied by Germany in the First World War. She helped British, French and Belgian soldiers escape and was arrested, tried and executed in 1915 by German authorities.

Curriculum link:

The lives of significant individuals.

THE ILLUSTRATED LONDON NEWS, OCT. 30, 1915.—547

"FAITH AND COURAGE IN DEATH": AN ALLEGORY OF EDITH CAVELL.
DRAWN BY A. FORESTIER.

"SHE DIED LIKE A HEROINE."

1 Drawing called 'Faith and courage in death, an allegory of Edith Cavell' from the *Illustrated London News*.

 Copyright © Clare Horrie and Rachel Hillman, 2020

🚀 Starter activity

Reveal the first source (the drawing from the *London Illustrated News*) as a mystery document to get the pupils thinking on the subject. Explain the words 'heroine' and 'allegory', as a picture with a hidden meaning. Ask the pupils:

- Who is the figure with wings?
- Who is lying on the ground?
- How would you describe the figure lying on the ground?
- Who stands in the darkness?
- Why are they there?
- What is the message of this picture?
- How do you think the British government used pictures like this to encourage people in Britain to support the war?

⭐ Main activity

Take a look at the second source (the statement from the Foreign Office) together. You can either print it out or project it on the whiteboard. Read the source aloud to pupils. Use the transcript on page 60 if needed. Highlight and define any difficult words.

Once pupils have understood the document, discuss the following questions as a class:

- What dangers did Edith Cavell face?
- Why do you think she acted?
- Are you surprised by her actions?
- Why were people shocked by how she was treated?
- Can you see a connection between the two sources?
- Why should we remember Edith Cavell?
- How do her role and achievements compare with those of Florence Nightingale?

🖊 Creative activity

Find a picture of the memorial to Edith Cavell in London and ask pupils to write their own inscription for it.

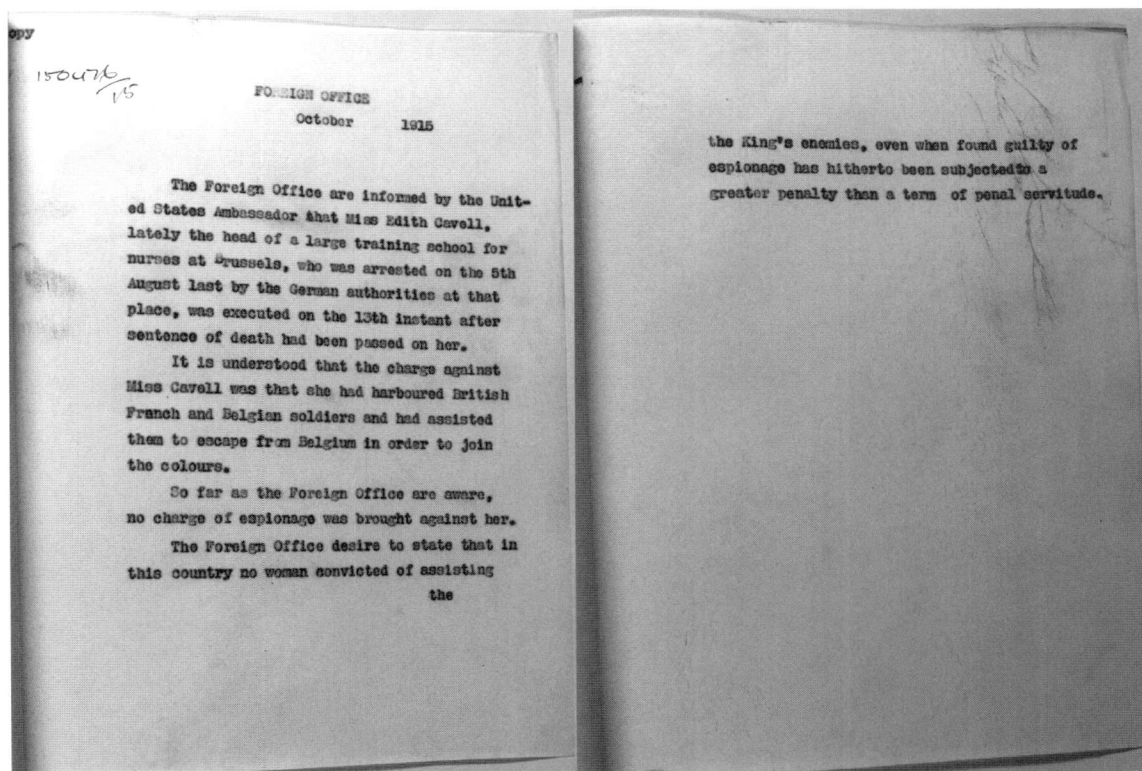

2 Statement issued from Foreign Office commenting on the execution of Edith Cavell.

📄 Transcript

Statement issued from Foreign Office commenting on the execution of Edith Cavell

FOREIGN OFFICE
October 1915

The Foreign Office are informed by the United States Ambassador that Miss Edith Cavell, lately the head of a large training school for nurses at Brussels, who was arrested on the 5th August last by the German authorities at that place, was executed on the 13th instant after sentence of death had been passed on her.

It is understood that the charge against Miss Cavell was that she had harboured British, French and Belgian soldiers and had assisted them to escape from Belgium in order to join the colours.

So far as the Foreign Office are aware, no charge of espionage was brought against her. The Foreign Office desire to state that in this country no woman convicted of assisting the King's enemies, even when found guilty of espionage has hitherto been subjected to a greater penalty than a term of penal servitude.

Copyright © Clare Horrie and Rachel Hillman, 2020

Emily Davison

↻ Lesson overview

Lesson enquiry question

Who was Emily Davison?

Resources required

Sources:

❶ Census entry for Emily Wilding Davison, 1911.

❷ Photograph of the King's horse, Anmer, being brought down by a suffragette.

Other:

· Worksheet: Design your own badge. Photocopy enough copies for one per pupil.

Lesson focus

Describe:

Describe who Emily Davison was.

Explain:

Explain that the suffragette movement was a campaign to get the vote for women.

Curriculum link:

The lives of significant individuals.

❶ Census entry for Emily Wilding Davison, 1911.

❷ Photograph of the King's horse, Anmer, being brought down by a suffragette.

🚀 Starter activity

Reveal the full image of the census as a mystery document. Set the timer to one minute and ask the pupils to tell you everything that they can spot before the time is up. Annotate the document image as they give their answers and encourage them to look at the document as an 'object', so that they consider the layout of the information on the page, including the fact that there is printed text alongside handwritten sections and that the size of the print varies (for example there is large print at the top to indicate the title).

Remove the image of the document for the moment, and run through the pupils' observations with them. Are there any words that they spotted? Do they know what these words mean? It is likely that the pupils will have spotted the title 'Census' at the top of the page.

Reveal the document image again, and ask them whether there is anything else that they now notice. If they haven't made this observation already, refer them to the title 'Census'. Do they know what a census is?

Explain that a census is a count of all the people in the United Kingdom on one particular day, and that it is taken every ten years. The first census in Britain was recorded in 1801 and there has been one every ten years since (apart from 1941 due to our involvement in the Second World War).

Draw the pupils' attention to the entry for Emily Wilding Davison. Can they work out her name? (Some of the pupils might have heard of her.) What was her age? Where was she born? Ask them to look at the entry for her occupation. What do they think occupation might mean? Emily was a political secretary; do the children have any idea what that might be?

Explain that Emily Davison was a suffragette, a member of a group that were fighting for women to have the vote. The suffragettes used 'actions' to make their case and to cause damage to property, for example setting fire to haystacks and postboxes. When the above census was taken, Emily Davison had hidden in a cupboard in the Chapel of Westminster so that she could record her residence (home) as the House of Commons!

Explain that the pupils are now going to find out more about Emily Davison by looking at another document.

⭐ Main activity

Ask the pupils to work in pairs and give them a copy of the second source (the photograph of the King's horse). Explain that they have a set time to work out the answers to the questions below. They can draw or write their answers, or just discuss in pairs.

- What type of document is this?
- What can you see in the image?
- What do you think has happened?
- What does this document have to do with Emily Davison?

Hear some of the pupils' answers, but don't comment at this stage.

Explain that Emily Davison is remembered for running in front of the King's horse at Epsom Derby in 1913, which resulted in her death. Ask:

- Why do you think she did this?

Explain that there is debate among historians about whether Emily Davison meant to hurt herself so badly, or if she just meant to cause a disruption. Whatever the case, she gave her life for the fight for women to have the vote – a cause that she (and many others) strongly believed in.

You could explain to pupils that some women got the vote at the end of the First World War in 1918, and that all women over the age of 21 received the vote in Britain in 1928.

✏️ Creative activity

Ask the pupils to design their own badges, like the suffragettes did in order to promote their cause. There are lots of images of suffrage badges available online for inspiration. Pupils could design a badge to promote a cause that they think is important, for example no homework or not wearing school uniform! You can photocopy and hand out the worksheet on page 63 to support this activity.

Copyright © Clare Horrie and Rachel Hillman, 2020

✏️ Worksheet: Design your own badge

The suffragettes campaigned for women to have the vote. Think about a cause that is really important to you. Design your own badge to promote your cause.

Why is this cause important to you?

_____

_____

_____

What have you included on your badge and why?

_____

_____

_____

Wright brothers air travel

⟳ Lesson overview

Lesson enquiry question

How did the Wright brothers change how we see the world?

Resources required

Source:

❶ Letter dated 10th April 1908 from the American Wright brothers to the UK War Office about a possible contract to build their two-man aeroplanes.

Other:

• Transcript for source 1.

Lesson focus

Describe:

Describe how Orville and Wilbur Wright were first to design and build a flying craft that could be controlled whilst in the air.

Explain:

Explain the significance of this invention.

Curriculum link:

The lives of significant individuals.

🚀 Starter activity

Begin the lesson with a class discussion on air travel. Ask:

• How did people travel before aeroplanes?
• How does flight change how we see the world?

Themes that you could guide pupils towards include:

• The boundaries that divide us can disappear.
• The distance between us shrinks and the horizon expands. The world is more connected.
• There are more possibilities for travel.
• We can learn more about our environment.
• Space exploration has been made possible.

⭐ Main activity

Reveal the source document to the class. Read it as a class and explain any difficult words. You can use the transcript on page 65 if needed. Once you are confident the pupils understand the text, ask them to discuss the following questions in pairs or small groups:

• Who is this letter from?
• Which country do the writers come from?
• Who are they writing to?
• How do they suggest their plane can be used?
• Why are the brothers writing to the British War Office?

Inspired by the Wright brothers' invention, pupils can now design their own type of transport. They should draw a diagram or picture, label it and write a short description of how their invention can be used.

✏ Creative activity

Pupils create an illustrated timeline of the Wright brothers. They can explore the primary sources on the Library of Congress website to help. See www.loc.gov/collections/wilbur-and-orville-wright-papers/about-this-collection.

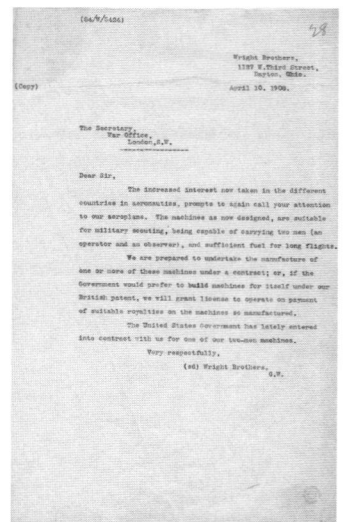

❶ Letter dated 10th April 1908 from the American Wright brothers to the UK War Office about a possible contract to build their two-man aeroplanes.

Copyright © Clare Horrie and Rachel Hillman, 2020

Transcript

Letter dated 10th April 1908 from the American Wright brothers to the UK War Office about a possible contract to build their two-man aeroplanes

(Copy)

Wright Brothers
1127 W. Third Street
Dayton, Ohio

April 10, 1908.

The Secretary
War Office
London, S.W.

Dear Sir,

The increased interest now taken in the different countries in aeronautics, prompts to again call your attention to our aeroplane. The machines as now designed, are suitable for military scouting, being capable of carrying two men (an operator and an observer) and sufficient fuel for long flights.

We are prepared to undertake the manufacture of one or more of these machines under a contract; or, if the Government would prefer to build machines for itself under our British patent, we will grant license to operate on payment of suitable royalties on the machines so manufactured.

The United States Government has lately entered into contract with us for one of our two-men machines.

Very respectfully,

(sd) Wright Brothers

O.W.

Winston Churchill

↻ Lesson overview

Lesson enquiry question

What is Winston Churchill famous for?

Resources required

Sources:

1. Photograph of Winston Churchill wearing a steel helmet.

2. Wings for Victory poster.

Other:

- Simplified transcript for source 2.

Lesson focus

Describe:

Describe who Winston Churchill was.

Explain:

Explain the role Winston Churchill played during the Second World War and why he was famous.

Curriculum link:

The lives of individuals who have contributed to national and international achievements.

MR. WINSTON CHURCHILL WEARING HIS STEEL HELMET & THE SMILE OF CONFIDENCE.

1 Photograph of Winston Churchill wearing a steel helmet.

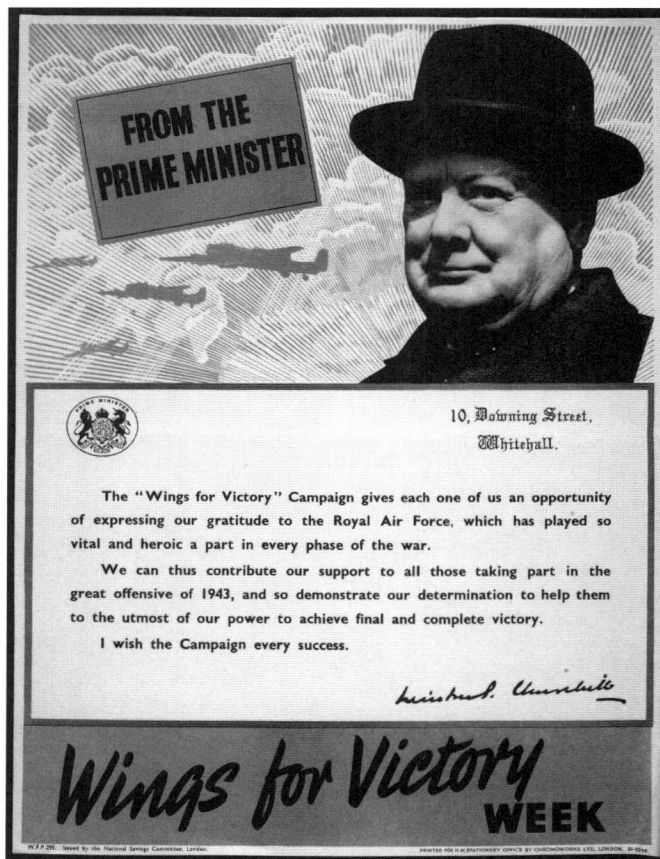

FROM THE PRIME MINISTER

10, Downing Street, Whitehall.

The "Wings for Victory" Campaign gives each one of us an opportunity of expressing our gratitude to the Royal Air Force, which has played so vital and heroic a part in every phase of the war.

We can thus contribute our support to all those taking part in the great offensive of 1943, and so demonstrate our determination to help them to the utmost of our power to achieve final and complete victory.

I wish the Campaign every success.

Winston S. Churchill

Wings for Victory WEEK

2 Wings for Victory poster.

Copyright © Clare Horrie and Rachel Hillman, 2020

🚀 Starter activity

Talk to the pupils about what it means to be famous. Can they all think of a person and why they are famous? You could write their ideas on the board, helping them to categorise the different reasons behind these people's fame, for example political leader, entertainer, sportsperson or helping others. Alternatively, you could give each group a set of cards with pictures of different famous people on them. Can they match the people up with the correct names and the correct job or role?

Once you've established the meaning of the term 'famous' and looked at some people who are famous today and why, explain to the pupils that they're now going to look at somebody who was famous in the past during the Second World War.

At this point, you can use a class timeline to help the pupils identify when the Second World War was. Explain that the person they are going to find out about was famous for doing a very important job during the war. This job was so special that we describe this person as significant; their role and their actions had an impact on lots of people living at this time.

Explain that you're now going to show them a photograph of this significant person. Reveal the photograph of Winston Churchill (with the caption blanked out) as a mystery document, and ask the pupils to spend five minutes chatting with a partner about how this person is dressed and what they think his job or role is.

Bring the pupils back together and ask them about the things that they've spotted. You could annotate a large image of the photograph projected on the whiteboard as they feed back their answers. Accept all answers as plausible at this stage.

- What have you noticed about this person's clothes?
- What job do you think this person did? Why do you think this?
- Have you any ideas about why he was important during the Second World War?
- Have you noticed anything else about the image? (Draw their attention to the blanked-out section of text.)

✏️ Creative activity

Ask the pupils to find out more about Winston Churchill. They could design a 'zine' (a mini magazine) using images from the documents and sourced from the internet, along with key words and phrases to convey information about Winston Churchill as a significant person.

- Why do you think this is here? What might it be hiding? (Explain that you have removed this section as it gives them further information about this person.)

Reveal the text and ask one of the pupils to read this aloud. What information does this give us about the famous person in the photograph? Why might he be wearing a 'smile of confidence'?

Explain that this person is called Winston Churchill and that he was the prime minister of Britain from 1940 until the end of the Second World War. He helped to rally the British people against the Nazis and he led the military planning and decision-making of the war. The caption describing his 'smile of confidence' suggests that Winston Churchill is showing everyone that he feels sure Britain will win the war. Why would it be important for him to show people that he is positive they will win?

⭐ Main activity

Now show the second document (the 'Wings for Victory' poster) with Winston Churchill's image and the text that reads 'From the Prime Minister'. Use the Spotlight tool or similar to hide the bottom section of the document with the text and line 'Wings for Victory'. Ask pupils the following:

- How would you describe Winston Churchill in this image?
- How is he dressed this time?
- What can you spot in the background next to him?
- What types of document are sent to someone from someone? Who might Churchill be sending this message to?

Now tell the pupils that you're going to show them the second part of the document. Hand out a copy of the document with the bottom section visible. Ask them to read the text aloud in pairs. Who is Winston Churchill writing to? What does he want them to do? A simplified transcript is supplied on page 68 if this would be more suited to your pupils' needs.

Bring the pupils back together and ask them to feed back their findings. Explain that 'Wings for Victory' was a fundraising campaign and nearly every town across the country had weeks where they were asked to contribute money for aeroplanes (for example a Spitfire, a Wellington or a Lancaster Bomber). Ask the pupils why supporting the RAF in this way was so important. Why would Winston Churchill be able to convince people to donate money for this cause?

Explain that at different points during the war, Britain's RAF had defended the country from invasion. Winston Churchill was a popular prime minister who was very good at raising people's morale (how positive they felt about winning the war), and because he was well liked, he was able to convince people to support this cause.

📄 Simplified transcript

'Wings for Victory'

From the Prime Minister

We can all say thank you to the Royal Air Force (RAF), by helping the 'Wings for Victory' campaign.

The Royal Air Force has played a very important part in the war. We can show our support and how much we want to win this war, by giving money to the RAF to help them fight.

Winston Churchill
Wings for Victory Week

Copyright © Clare Horrie and Rachel Hillman, 2020

Nelson Mandela

⟳ Lesson overview

Lesson enquiry question

Why should we remember Nelson Mandela?

Resources required

Source:

❶ Letter of thanks from Nelson Mandela (1918–2013) to Sir John Maud for sending him books via the British Embassy, 14th September 1962.

Other:

- Transcript for source 1.
- Topic books on Nelson Mandela.

Lesson focus

Describe:

Describe who Nelson Mandela was and why we should remember him.

Explain:

Explain where South Africa is located on a map or globe.

Curriculum link:

The lives of significant individuals.

❶ Letter of thanks from Nelson Mandela (1918–2013) to Sir John Maud for sending him books via the British Embassy, 14th September 1962.

🚀 Starter activity

Introduce the pupils to Nelson Mandela. Explain that he was a South African political leader who fought against the injustice in the country that took away the basic rights of black South Africans and prevented them from governing themselves. He became the first black president of South Africa and was awarded the Nobel Peace Prize. He was imprisoned for 27 years by the white minority government because of his fight against segregation.

As a class, use the topic books or online dictionaries to find the meanings of the following key words, which relate to Nelson Mandela's life:

- South Africa
- human rights
- racial prejudice
- peace
- segregation
- apartheid
- life sentence
- hard labour
- Nobel Peace Prize
- president.

⭐ Main activity

Reveal the source document to the class. Discuss it with the pupils and explain any difficult words. Once the pupils understand the text, ask them to discuss the following questions in pairs or small groups. You can provide pupils with a copy of the transcript on page 71 if required.

- Who is this letter from?
- Who is he writing to?
- Why is this person writing?
- Why did Nelson Mandela appreciate receiving these books?
- What does this letter show about Nelson Mandela as a person?
- What does it show about his beliefs?

Once the pupils have discussed these questions in their pairs or groups, ask them to feed back their findings to the rest of the class.

✏️ Creative activity

Using the topic books or by researching online, pupils create an illustrated poster that explains how Nelson Mandela wanted to change South Africa. The poster could show information such as:

- Nelson Mandela wanted to make the country a fairer place to live in, as the smaller white population were in charge of the country at the time.
- Black people were forced to live separate lives. They could not use the same schools, hospitals, beaches and shops as white people.
- Conditions in whites-only schools and hospitals were much better.
- White and black people in South Africa lived separate lives under a system called apartheid.
- Black people were denied basic rights, like being allowed to vote in elections or have freedom of speech.
- Nelson Mandela believed that everybody should be treated equally.

Copyright © Clare Horrie and Rachel Hillman, 2020

📄 Transcript

Letter of thanks from Nelson Mandela to Sir John Maud for sending him books via the British Embassy, 14th September 1962

Nelson Mandela (1918–2013) was a South African anti-apartheid political leader who was to serve as the first black president of South Africa and was awarded the Nobel Peace Prize. He was imprisoned for 27 years by the government because of his fight against apartheid.

```
The Jail
Johannesburg
14th September 1962

Sir John Maud GCB, CBE
The British Embassy
No 6 The Street
Pretoria

Dear Sir,

I have received the six books which were
sent to me by a friend in England through
your Embassy. I thank you for making it
possible for me to receive them, and I should
be grateful if you would kindly inform the
friend, should you be in possession of his or
her address, that I greatly appreciate this
valuable present.

Yours faithfully

N. Mandela
NELSON MANDELA
AWAITING TRIAL PRISONER

13260/62
```

Cenotaph commemoration

◉ Lesson overview

Lesson enquiry question

Why do we remember the First World War?

Resources required

Sources:

❶ Extracts from a document written in 1930 explaining the planning and building of the Cenotaph in London.

❷ Page from the *Illustrated London News*, 26th July 1919.

Other:

• Transcripts of sources 1 and 2.

Lesson focus

Describe:

Describe the first commemoration for the First World War and commemoration now.

Explain:

Explain the term cenotaph from the Greek, which means an empty tomb or monument.

Curriculum link:

Significant historical events, people and places in pupils' own locality.

There was no time to be lost. The Office of Works called me into consultation and requested me to submit a design. I did so at once, and my original drawing, now in the Imperial War Museum, shows what the Cenotaph was like when it first shaped itself on paper before me. I called it a Cenotaph, conveying the simple meaning of an Empty Tomb up-lifted on High Pedestal.

PLAN APPROVED

The plan was approved, and the Cenotaph, at first a structure of wood and plaster, was erected on its present site in Whitehall, where it figures in the unforgettable Peace Procession of July, 1919. Crowds began to assemble at break of dawn, many theatres were closed on account of traffic congestion, and no less than 1,500 officers and 15,000 other ranks had to camp under canvas to enable them to take part in that memorable ceremony.

A PERMANENT MONUMENT

It was proposed that near the end of the Horse Guards Parade would be a suitable site, and the permanence of the Cenotaph was raised in Parliament by Captain Ormsby Gore, M.P., who suggested that the memorial should be "erected in Portland stone". When it thus became evident that public opinion had decided on a permanent monument, the question of a fresh design was canvassed. One, I remember, was put forward by a nobleman of high standing in the political world. His idea was for a great granite cross, with the Union Jack proudly prominent in the design. Other ideas were talked about, but got no further than words.

Time passed, and the plain fact emerged and grew stronger every hour that the Cenotaph was what the people wanted, and that they wanted to have the wood and plaster original replaced by an identical memorial in lasting stone. It was a mass-feeling too deep to express itself more fitly than by the piles of ever-fresh flowers which loving hands placed on the Cenotaph day by day. Thus it was decided, by the human sentiment of millions, that the Cenotaph should be as it now is, and speaking as the designer, I could wish for no greater honour, no more complete and lasting satisfaction.

"THE GLORIOUS DEAD"

"The glorious dead", the words I put on my original sketch, also survived unchanged. Prebendary Carlile, of the Church Army, suggested:

❶ Extracts from a document written in 1930 explaining the planning and building of the Cenotaph in London.

Copyright © Clare Horrie and Rachel Hillman, 2020

🚀 Starter activity

Look at both extracts in the first source (the document explaining the planning and building of the Cenotaph) together and explain any difficult words. Discuss the following with the pupils as a class:

- What does the word 'cenotaph' mean?
- What was the first cenotaph made of?
- What happened at the first Peace Procession?
- Why did people want a permanent cenotaph?
- What type of design did the people want?
- Why do you think the Cenotaph had such simple words on it?

⭐ Main activity

Print out copies of the second source (the newspaper article) or project a large version of it on the whiteboard. Read the top caption aloud and discuss the following questions with the pupils:

- What are you looking at?
- Can you spot:
  - the guardsmen
  - General Haig
  - some flags
  - a wreath?
- What is happening in this scene?
- Does the Cenotaph appear to be a suitable and respectful memorial?
- Was the ceremony well attended by the British public?

Now read the article below the photograph with the pupils. Use the transcript on page 75 to help if necessary. Ask pupils the following questions:

- Can you think of other sources that could help us find out more about commemoration in 1919?
- Why do you think the First World War has been commemorated annually for 100 years?
- Why does this commemoration include other wars to the present day?
- Why is it important to remember?
- Could we remember past conflicts in a different way?

📝 Creative activity

Pupils make a display of photographs of other war memorials including the Cenotaph today. You may have a local memorial that you could introduce to pupils and you can also mention other memorials at Thiepval in France or the Menin Gate in Ypres. Discuss with pupils the continued form of commemoration of the First World War with the poppy as artefact.

2 Page from the *Illustrated London News*, 26th July 1919.

Transcript

Extracts from a document written in 1930 called 'The story of the Cenotaph', told by Sir Edwin Lutyens the architect and artist who designed it

Extract 1

There was no time to be lost. The Office of Works called me into consultation and requested me to submit a design. I did so at once, and my original drawing, now in the Imperial War Museum, shows what the Cenotaph was like when it first shaped itself on paper before me. I called it a Cenotaph, conveying the simple meaning of an Empty Tomb uplifted on High Pedestal.

PLAN APPROVED

The plan was approved, and the Cenotaph, at first a structure of wood and plaster, was erected on its present site in Whitehall, where it figures in the unforgettable Peace Procession of July, 1919. Crowds began to assemble at break of dawn, many theatres were closed on account of traffic congestion, and no less than 1,500 officers and 15,000 other ranks had to camp under canvas to enable them to take part in that memorable ceremony.

Extract 2

A PERMAMENT MONUMENT

It was proposed that near the end of the Horse Guards Parade would be a suitable site, and the permanence of the Cenotaph was raised in Parliament by Captain Ormsby Gore, M.P., who suggested that the memorial should be "erected in Portland stone". When it became evident that public opinion had decided on a permanent monument, the question of a fresh design was canvassed. One, I remember, was put forward by a nobleman of high standing in the political world. His idea was for a great granite cross, with the Union Jack proudly prominent in the design. Other ideas were talked about, but got no further than words.

Time passed, and the plain fact emerged and grew stronger every hour that the Cenotaph was what the people wanted, and that they wanted to have the wood and plaster original replaced by an identical memorial in lasting stone. It was a mass-feeling too deep to express itself more fitly than by the piles of ever-fresh flowers which loving hands placed on the Cenotaph day by day. Thus it was decided, by the human sentiment of millions, that the Cenotaph should be as it now is, and speaking as the designer, I could wish for no greater honour, no more complete and lasting satisfaction.

"THE GLORIOUS DEAD"

"The glorious dead", the words I put on my original sketch, also survived unchanged.

 Copyright © Clare Horrie and Rachel Hillman, 2020

Transcript

The *Illustrated London News*, July 26th 1919

The Glorious Dead: Sir Douglas Haig Saluting
Drawn by Our Special Artist, A. Forestier

Symbolising the true spirit of the peace celebrations: The Cenotaph in Whitehall to "the Glorious Dead"- Sir Douglas Haig (left foreground) saluting it as he rode by.

The mood of rejoicing over the victorious end of such a war as we have gone through was tempered, in thousands of hearts, by the remembrance of the dead whose sacrifice made the victory possible. These thoughts were duly symbolised in the fine Cenotaph erected in the middle of Whitehall to commemorate the men and women who died in the service of their country. The monument embodied the true spirit of the occasion. It had been arranged that, as the troops approached it in the procession, they should divide into two columns and march past at the salute, those on the right with "eyes left", and those on the left with "eyes right". Owing, however, to a movement of the great crowd, which there was no time to alter, there was no space left on the right of the Cenotaph, and the procession passed without dividing. The memorial, designed by Sir Edwin Lutyens, consisted of a simple pylon 33 ft. high. On either side were arranged groups of flags. Above the three steps of the base was carved: "The Glorious Dead, 1914-1919." At the top of the column was placed an altar containing a brazier. At each corner stood a Guardsman with arms reversed.

Christmas in the First World War

⟳ Lesson overview

Lesson enquiry question

Did the First World War stop at Christmas?

Resources required

Sources:

❶ Extract from a report in war diary of 15th Infantry Brigade to Headquarters describing events of Christmas Eve and Christmas Day, 1914.

❷ Letter from A. Maggs, B.E.F. 20th December 1915.

❸ Letter extract from Arthur Smith, Royal Engineers, III Corps Railhead, B.E.F. January 1916.

Sources 2 and 3 are examples of some of the many letters sent by staff of the Great Western Railway Audit Office at Paddington who had enlisted to fight in the First World War.

Other:

· Transcripts for sources 1, 2 and 3.

Lesson focus

Describe:

Describe what happened on some parts of the Western Front on Christmas Eve and Christmas Day in 1914.

Explain:

Explain that this was not a permanent ceasefire and other sources show how Christmas was celebrated by soldiers in 1915.

Curriculum link:

Significant historical events.

❶ Extract from a report in war diary of 15th Infantry Brigade to Headquarters describing events of Christmas Eve and Christmas Day, 1914.

Copyright © Clare Horrie and Rachel Hillman, 2020

🚀 Starter activity

Reveal the first source (the extract from the war diary report) as a mystery document. Explain any difficult words given in square brackets within the transcript if needed. Discuss the following questions with the pupils:

- How many British soldiers met with German soldiers?
- Why do you think this happened?
- What did they do when they met?
- Why do you think the Germans did not 'talk shop'?
- How long did the Germans say the war would last?
- When did the British decide to start firing again?

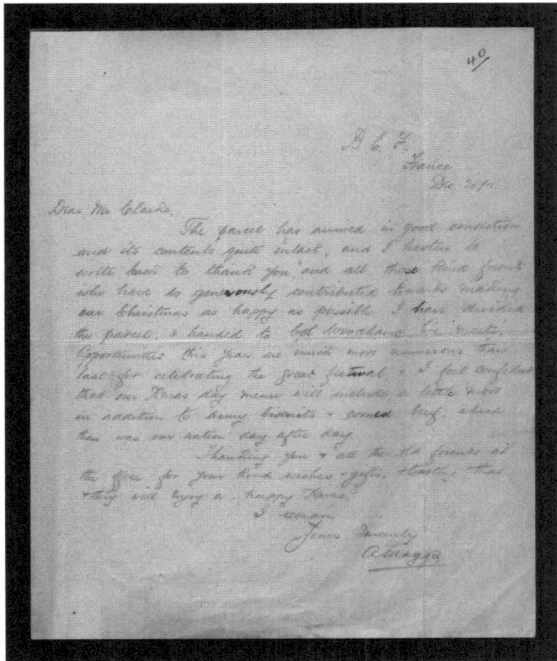

② Letter from A. Maggs, B.E.F. 20th December 1915.

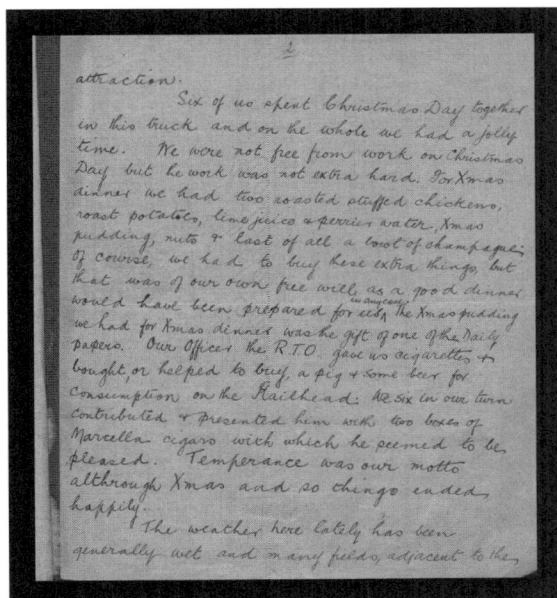

③ Letter extract from Arthur Smith, Royal Engineers, III Corps Railhead, B.E.F. January 1916.

⭐ Main activity

Explain to pupils that you will now explore two other sources from the following year that show how Christmas was celebrated in the First World War.

Divide the class into groups. Give half the groups one of the letters and give the remaining groups the other letter. Can they find out the following?

- Who wrote their letter?
- What is the date?
- What did some soldiers have for Christmas dinner?
- What did soldiers usually eat?
- Is there anything that surprises you about the letter?
- What do you have for Christmas dinner? Is it very different?
- Why are these letters different from the starter mystery document?
- Which is more useful to find out about Christmas in the First World War?

Ask the groups to feed back their findings to the rest of the class. Can each letter answer all of the questions? Why is it good to have more than one source?

🖊 Creative activity

Make a suitable selection from some of the other soldiers' letters (with transcripts) found at the following links:

www.nationalarchives.gov.uk/education/resources/letters-first-world-war-1915

www.nationalarchives.gov.uk/education/resources/letters-first-world-war-1916-18

Read the selection together. Now ask pupils to work in pairs or individually to write a soldier's letter home. You can create a class display with the letters.

Copyright © Clare Horrie and Rachel Hillman, 2020

Transcript

Extract from a report in war diary of 15th Infantry Brigade to Headquarters describing events of Christmas Eve and Christmas Day, 1914

Note: 'Norfolks' and 'Cheshires' were the names of particular regiments linked to particular counties in the UK. The infantry is the branch of an army that carries out military combat on foot, unlike cavalry or tank forces.

Some words defined in [square brackets].

Headquarters,
5th Division

_____

I beg to report that an informal meeting took place yesterday between the lines of trenches of ourselves and the Germans, at which about 200 of our men assisted, and an even larger number of Germans.

It appears that on Christmas Eve there was a good deal of shouting and chaff [joking/banter] between our right trenches (Norfolks) and the Germans about LA PETITE DOUVE Farm, each inviting the other to come over. Although there was a certain amount of firing on our part all yesterday morning and up to 2 p.m. (Christmas Day), there was no response of rifle fire from the enemy on our front (only a few shells in the early morning some distance to the North). About 2 p.m. a German Officer or N.C.O. [Non Commissioned Officer – a soldier who did not lead men] appeared and walked over to our trenches holding up a box of cigars. He was not fired at, and one or two of our men went to meet him. Others, German and Englishmen, chimed [joined] in and soon there were large numbers in the space between the trenches nearer the German ones than to ours, talking and fraternizing [being friendly] and accepting each other's cigars and cigarettes etc. Most of the Norfolks and some of the Cheshires (on their left) from the fire trenches took part in this informal gathering including several officers.

The latter reported that the Germans refused to talk "shop" but were very friendly and appeared to have no evil intention of any sort. They said the war would be over and ourselves beaten, in two months and said they hadn't begun in earnest [started fighting their hardest] yet, although we had the best of them up to the present [we had been winning at the moment]. They also showed an official memo [message] stating that the Russians had been smashed and were fleeing to WARSAW, also the Austrians had occupied BELGRADE.

…

26/12/14   Sd. Gleichen, Brigadier General.

                                 Commanding 15th Infantry Brigade

P.S. The Germans stated that they were not taking any action by fire or otherwise from 25th to 27th instant. I have however ordered hostilities [firing of guns] to proceed [continue] as usual.

 Copyright © Clare Horrie and Rachel Hillman, 2020

📄 Transcript

Letter from A. Maggs, B.E.F. 20th December 1915

B.E.F.
France
December 20/15

Dear Mr. Clarke,

The parcel has arrived in good condition and its contents quite intact [not damaged], and I hasten to write back to thank you and all those kind friends who have so generously contributed towards making our Christmas as happy as possible. I have divided the parcel and handed to Corporal Woodhams his 'moiety' [share]. Opportunities this year are much more numerous than last for celebrating the great festival and I feel confident that our Xmas day menu will include a little more in addition to army biscuits and corned beef, which then was our ration day after day.

Thanking you and all the old friends at the office for your kind wishes and gifts and trusting that they will enjoy a happy Xmas,

I remain yours sincerely,

A. Maggs

Transcript

Letter extract from Arthur Smith, Royal Engineers, III Corps Railhead, B.E.F. January 1916

Note: The following letter extract is from a soldier based at a railhead. This is a point behind the frontline trenches where railways, used to transport men, supplies and ammunition, met. As it was behind the line, men stationed there would sometimes go to nearby villages to get other food supplies. This soldier would have split his time between the railhead station and the frontline trenches. Working at the railhead he would have been involved in laying and fixing tracks and cables, loading and unloading supplies, transporting supplies to the frontline and so on.

Six of us spent Christmas Day together in this truck and on the whole we had a jolly time. We were not free from work on Christmas Day but the work was not extra hard. For Xmas dinner we had two roasted stuffed chickens, roast potatoes, lime juice and Perrier water [fizzy water], Xmas pudding, nuts and last of all a bowl of champagne. Of course, we had to buy these extra things, but that was of our own free will as a good dinner would have been prepared for us in any case. The Xmas pudding we had for Xmas dinner was the gift of one of the Daily papers. Our Officer the R.T.O. [Railway Transport Officer] gave us cigarettes and bought, or helped to buy, a pig and some beer for consumption on the Railhead. We six in our turn contributed and presented him with two boxes of Marcella cigars with which he seemed to be pleased. Temperance [not too much drinking alcohol] was our motto all through Xmas and so things ended happily.

The weather here lately has been generally wet ….

Copyright © Clare Horrie and Rachel Hillman, 2020

Census

↻ Lesson overview

Lesson enquiry question

Why is a census important?

Resources required

Sources:

❶ Census return for Buckingham Palace, 1851.

❷ Census return for Westminster, 1851.

Other:

- Simplified transcripts for sources 1 and 2.
- Worksheet: Census return. Photocopy one per pupil.

Lesson focus

Describe:

Describe what a census is.

Explain:

Explain why a census is an important record.

Curriculum link:

Significant historical events, people and places in pupils' own locality.

❶ Census return for Buckingham Palace, 1851.

❷ Census return for Westminster, 1851.

🚀 Starter activity

Explain to the pupils that you are going to give them a mystery document to look at. They can work in pairs or small groups, but they only have five minutes to find out as much as they possibly can!

Give each group an enlarged copy of the first census document. Ask them to see if they can answer the following questions and encourage them to annotate the document as they work:

- What does the document look like? For example, is it handwritten or typed? Are there lots of lines of text or is the text set out in a specific way?
- Can you read any of the words?
- Can you spot the names of any famous people?
- What type of document might this be?

Bring the pupils back together and ask them about the things that they've spotted. You could annotate a large image of the census projected on the whiteboard as they feed back their answers.

Explain to the pupils that they have been looking at a document that was made in 1851. Do they know who was queen at this time? Can they find 1851 on the class timeline? Explain that this document is called a census. This is a count of everyone in the United Kingdom on a particular day. The first census took place in 1801 and there has been one held every ten years since then (apart from 1941 during the Second World War). Return to the image of the census on the whiteboard.

Using the simplified transcript if helpful, or just by taking a section of the census, encourage the pupils to be more analytical now. Can they see whose census return is shown here? Who is listed as the head of the household (the person 'in charge')? What is this person's title? Where was this family staying at the time of the census? How many children are listed and what does this tell us about the size of the family? Who else is listed apart from the family and why have they been included?

Explain that this census return is for Queen Victoria and her family! Even though she was the queen of England, her husband Albert is still shown as the head of the household. What does this tell us about the way in which women were viewed in Victorian times? All of the people listed apart from the family are servants. Queen Victoria would have had a lot of servants to help cook and clean Buckingham Palace, as well as to dress the family and to provide advice and education.

The census is still taken today and is used by the government to gather information on people living in the UK at a particular time.

⭐ Main activity

Explain to the pupils that after 1851 the census contained even more information than it had done in the past. We can use it to find out about people's ages, where they were born and their relationship within the family (such as wife, mother and so on).

Give them a copy of the second census to look at in pairs or small groups, along with the simplified transcript if helpful. Tell them that this census return is also from Westminster but a different part. Ask them to discuss the following questions in groups:

- Can you spot some of the different jobs that men are listed as doing? Do any of these jobs not exist today? Why not?
- What jobs did women do at this time?
- Can you find an individual that interests you and find out their age, job and where they were born?

Bring the pupils back together and ask them to feed back their findings. Why do they think that a census can be an important piece of information for a historian?

To encourage pupils to think about history in their local area, you could ask the pupils to look at a particular street in their neighbourhood over a period of 30 years in three versions of the census, such as 1861, 1871 and 1881. How have families and their circumstances changed over this time?

You can find out more about viewing census records at www.nationalarchives.gov.uk/records/census-records.htm. (There is a small fee to download census documents, but they can be searched free of charge.)

✏️ Creative activity

Ask the pupils to conduct their own mini census returns by asking their friends about the different people living in their homes and what their jobs or roles are. They could record this information on their very own census return sheets! You can use the worksheet on page 85 to support this activity.

Copyright © Clare Horrie and Rachel Hillman, 2020

Simplified transcript

Census return for Buckingham Palace, 1851

Parish of St George Hanover Square | City of Westminster

No. on census	Name of Street, Place, or Road, and Name or No. of House	Name and Surname of each Person who abode in the house, on the Night of the 30th March, 1851	Relation to Head of Family	Condition [Married or not]	Age of		Rank, Profession, or Occupation	Where Born	Whether Blind, or Deaf-and-Dumb
					Males	Females			
1	Buckingham Palace	Her Majesty Alexandrina Victoria	Wife	Mar		31	The Queen	Kensington Palace	
		H.R.H. Francis Albert Augustus Charles Emanuel	Head	Mar	31		Duke of Saxony, Prince of Coburg and Gotha		
		H.R.H. Victoria Adelaide Mary Louisa	Dau			10	Princess Royal	Buckingham Palace	
		H.R.H. Albert Edward	Son		9		Prince of Wales	Do	
		H.R.H. Alice Maud Mary	Dau			7	Princess	Do	
		H.R.H. Alfred Ernest Albert	Son		6		Prince of United Kingdom. Duke of Saxony Prince of Coburg and Gotha	Windsor Castle	
		H.R.H. Helena Augusta Victoria	Dau			4	Princess	Buckingham Palace	
		H.R.H. Louisa Caroline Alberta	Dau			3	Princess	Do	
		H.R.H. Arthur William Patrick Albert	Son		1m		Prince of United Kingdom. Duke of Saxony Prince of Coburg and Gotha	Do	
2	Buckingham Palace	Amelia Matilda Murray		U		55	Maid of Honor	Kent Hunton	
		Lucy Maria Kerr		U		28	Do	Scotland Edinburgh	
		Mary Percy		U		32	Servant to do	Dorset Blandford	
		Lydia Gratner		U		28	Wardrobe Maid	Derby Derby	
		Selina Lindfield		U		28	Princess Royal's Draper	Berkshire Sunninghill	
Total of Houses			Total of Persons		4	10			

▤ Simplified transcript

Census return for Westminster, 1851

Parish of St George Hanover Square   Ecclesiastical District of St Peters   City of Westminster

No. on census	Name of Street, Place, or Road, and Name or No. of House	Name and Surname of each Person who abode in the house, on the Night of the 30th March, 1851	Relation to Head of Family	Condition [Married or not]	Age of Males	Age of Females	Rank, Profession, or Occupation	Where Born	Whether Blind, or Deaf-and-Dumb
1	20 Brewer St	Thomas Greenwood	Head	Mar	65		Stonemason	Hereford	
		Anna Do	wife	Mar		48	Laundress	Gloucestershire Cheltenham	
2		Mary Froude	widow			51	Lodging House Keeper	Cornwall St Cullam	
		John Froude	Son	U	14		Errand boy	London St Brides	
		William Bailey	Lodger	U	38		Labourer	Devon Modbury	
		Henry Ayling	Lodger	U	25		Coachman	Surrey Guildford	
		William Ayling	Lodger	U	28		Labourer	Surrey Guildford	
3		Edward Young	Head	Mar	29		Carpenter	Surrey Clapham	
		Elizabeth Ann Young	wife	Mar		29	Straw Bonnet Maker	Hants Gosport	
		Edward Young	Son		5			Surrey Lambeth	
		Harriet Young	Dau			1 month		Middlesex Pimlico	
4		Martha Brown	wife	Mar		41	Chandler's Shop Keeper	Surrey Lambeth	
		Thomas Brown	Son		11		Scholar	Middlesex Pimlico	
		Emily Brown	Dau					Do	
5		John Barber	Head	Mar	41		Bricklayer	Suffolk Framlingham	
		Mary Ann Barber	wife	Mar		32	Bricklayers wife	Suffolk Stowmarket	
		Frederick Barber	Son		10		Scholar	Westminster St Johns	
		Maria Barber	Dau			2 months	Scholar	Middlesex Pimlico	
Total of Houses		Total of Persons			10	8			

Copyright © Clare Horrie and Rachel Hillman, 2020

Worksheet: Census return

Ask three friends about the people who live in their homes. Record the information in the census return.

No. on Census	Address	Name and Surname of each Person in the House	Relation to Head of Family	Age of Males	Age of Females	Rank, Profession, or Occupation	Where Born
1							
2							
3							
4							
5							
6							
7							
8							

Copyright © Clare Horrie and Rachel Hillman, 2020

Industrial Revolution

⟳ Lesson overview

Lesson enquiry question

What were conditions like for Victorian children working in the mines?

Resources required

Sources:

❶ Photograph of a Victorian mine.

❷ Report of Employment Commission: illustration and John Saville's interview.

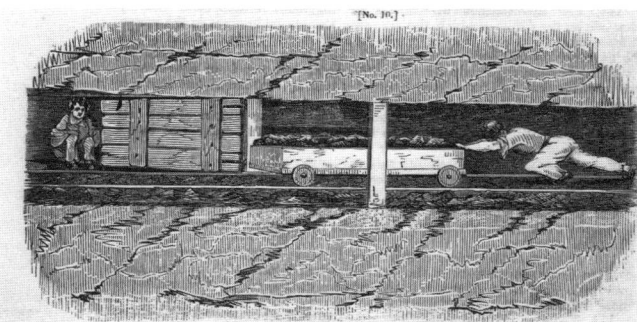

Other:

- Simplified transcript for John Saville's interview in source 2.
- Handling items: fake coal, smell pot (coal-burning fire).

Lesson focus

Describe:

Describe what a mine is.

Explain:

Explain the different types of work that children did in a mine and why it was dangerous.

Curriculum link:

Significant historical events, people and places in pupils' own locality.

❶ Photograph of a Victorian mine.

❷ (Below and right) Report of Employment Commission: illustration and John Saville's interview.

Copyright © Clare Horrie and Rachel Hillman, 2020

🚀 Starter activity

Explain to the pupils that you are going to show them a mystery document. They will have one minute to look at the photograph and discuss with a partner all of the different things that they can spot. Show the image of the Victorian mine on the whiteboard. After 60 seconds remove the image.

Ask the pupils to tell you everything that they remember spotting in the photograph and scribe their ideas on the board. Do they have any idea about where this photograph is set or what this place might have been used for? Accept all answers as plausible at this point.

Now display the document image again on the whiteboard. What did they miss the first time around? Highlight any of the details that they've missed on the image. Return to the previous questions about where they think this photograph is set and what they think this place was used for. Encourage them to look at the roof and floor of the image. What can they see? What might this rock have been used for?

Tell the pupils that they have been looking at a photograph that was taken in Victorian times, when Queen Victoria was on the throne. (You could use the class timeline here to help the pupils understand when this was.) Explain that this document shows a place called a coal mine. Have any of the children come across coal before or do they understand what it was used for? At this point you could use some 'fake' coal for the children to pass round (a rock painted with black paint and varnished works well!). You could also use a smell pot to help the children understand the smoky smell of coal fires.

Explain that during Victorian times, people burnt coal in fireplaces to heat their homes (before we had central heating). Coal also played a very important role in the factories that were being built across the country. Their new machinery was powered by steam, and coal was the fuel that was used to create the steam. Coal was also used in the steam engines of the new trains that were enabling people to travel from place to place. As there was such a big demand for coal at this time, more coal mines were being established and they mined deeper and deeper underground for the coal. Ask the children who they think might have worked in these coal mines and what sorts of jobs they might they have done.

✏️ Creative activity

Ask the pupils to create mini freeze-frames of work and conditions inside the mines.

Explain to the children that you're now going to give them another document: a picture that shows people working deep underground in the mines. In pairs or small groups, can they describe what they can see and what they think the people are doing?

Once the pupils have had time to look at the image in pairs or small groups, encourage them to feed back their answers. Explain that these people are working as trappers in the mine – this meant that they sat in the tunnels and opened and closed the ventilation doors for the coal wagons to pass through. Ask the pupils whether they think this would have been a pleasant job. Why or why not? Ask them to look at the image again and focus on the person sitting in the tunnel. What do they notice? If they haven't observed this already, explain to them that this person is a child and that trappers were children, sometimes as young as six or seven years of age. The tunnels would have been very narrow (the space underneath the pupils' tables is a good way to illustrate the height of some of these tunnels), and they would have been dark, hot and sometimes very damp places.

⭐ Main activity

Explain to the pupils that they're now going to use another document to find out what it was really like for children working as trappers in the mines. Explain that in 1842 the government investigated conditions in mines for children and, as part of this enquiry, they spoke to lots of different children about their experiences and recorded this information in a huge report (Report of the Children's Commission of 1842).

In pairs, give pupils the extract of John Saville's interview and the simplified transcript. Encourage them to read through this together, focussing on what they do understand. Where was John working? What does he think of his work? What are the conditions like?

Bring the pupils back together and ask them to feed back their findings. Explore the following questions:

- Was there anything that surprised them in the document? Why?
- Do they think that it was fair to employ children in this way? Why or why not?

Explain that for many poorer people in Victorian times, sending their children out to work meant that they could afford to feed them and keep a roof over their heads. It was a necessity. There were also other jobs for children apart from work in the coal mines, such as the factories, chimney sweeps, scavengers and so on. As a further research project, the pupils could find out about other types of work children did in Victorian times and what conditions were like in these roles.

Copyright © Clare Horrie and Rachel Hillman, 2020

▤ Simplified transcript

Interview with John Saville

No. 7 John Saville, 7 years old, collier's boy [coal miner] at the Soap Put. Interviewed January 19th

I've worked in the pit for two weeks. I open and shut the door. I'm normally in the dark and I sit down against the door. I like the work well enough; it doesn't make me tired. I work for 12 hours in the coal mine, and I never see daylight now except on Sundays. They don't treat me badly or beat me. I fell asleep one day and a corve [coal wagon] ran over my leg and made it hurt.

When I get home, I wash myself and have something to eat and drink. I drink tea and sometimes dry bread, or sometimes bread and cheese. I sometimes have red herring and potatoes for my dinner in the pit [coal mine]. I eat four times a day in the pit. I don't know my letters. I've never been to school at all. I go to Sunday School and I go to chapel [church] on a Sunday. I don't know who made the world and I don't know about God.

Inspector's note:
This boy cannot write or tell one letter.

Copyright © Clare Horrie and Rachel Hillman, 2020

Life in a rural locality

Lesson overview

Lesson enquiry question

What was life like in the country over 100 years ago and how can photographs help us find out?

Resources required

Sources:

❶ Photograph by P. H. Emerson showing women working in the fields, 1886.

❷ Photograph by P. H. Emerson showing girls osier-peeling, or removing the bark from willow rods used to make baskets, 1887.

❸ Photograph by P. H. Emerson, showing brick making, 1887.

Lesson focus

Describe:

Describe how photographs can help us to find out about the past.

Explain:

Explain that P. H. Emerson (1856–1936) was a photographer who specialised in rural subjects (in East Anglia) and wanted to record nature as truthfully as possible. He felt that people should be photographed in their own environment, rather than having to wear costumes and be placed in front of fake backgrounds, which was popular at the time.

Curriculum link:

Significant historical events, people and places in pupils' own locality.

❶ Photograph by P. H. Emerson showing women working in the fields, 1886.

Copyright © Clare Horrie and Rachel Hillman, 2020

🚀 Starter activity

Show pupils source 1. Discuss with them the following:

- What type of source is this?
- What does the source tell us about farm work?
- How hard was this work and can you explain why?
- Why was this photograph taken?
- How can it tell us about life in the past?
- How has farming changed?

2 Photograph by P. H. Emerson showing girls osier-peeling, or removing the bark from willow rods used to make baskets, 1887.

⭐ Main activity

Now show the whole class sources 2 and 3. Compare and contrast the two photographs, framing the discussion using the following questions:

- What can you see?
- What are the people doing in each photograph?
- How are the photographs different?
- What is the significance of these photographs?
- How do both tell us about life in the past?
- How have jobs and ways of working changed since these photographs were taken?

✍️ Creative activity

Ask pupils to make a collection of other sources to find out about farming today and share them with the rest of the class. Look at these sources alongside the three historical sources used in this lesson and, as a class, make a list of the differences you can see.

If possible, take a look with your class at the census for your area for 1881–1891 (see page 81) and find out more about the different jobs people did at that time in your region.

3 Photograph by P. H. Emerson, showing brick making, 1887.

Copyright © Clare Horrie and Rachel Hillman, 2020

Part 2
Key Stage 2

Introduction to Key Stage 2: Developing historical skills and chronological understanding

The lessons in this section are designed to use with Key Stage 2 pupils and will allow teachers to continue to develop their pupils' skills in history by increasing their confidence in using sources. This will support their enquiry skills, such as their questioning techniques and their powers of evaluation and appreciation of historical perspective. The activities can be used to support National Curriculum requirements to build chronological understanding. There are lessons that encourage pupils to make connections and contrasts and examine trends over time, as well as compose their own historical questions about change, cause, similarity and difference, and significance. The lessons allow pupils to construct their own responses that are based on evidence and argument and organisation of relevant historical material. Again, this process helps them to understand how our knowledge of the past is based on a range of sources. Finally, the curriculum aims of 'overview' and 'depth in historical study' are accommodated within these teaching materials as part of any scheme of work.

The main connections to the curriculum in this section of the book provide lessons based on topics including Bronze Age technology, the Roman Empire and its army, Roman gods, Anglo-Saxon art and culture, Alfred the Great and Edward the Confessor. There are activities based on the changing power of monarchs using case studies on King John and Magna Carta, and Queen Anne. The lessons also cover an aspect of social history from past to present based on crime and punishment and significant turning points in British history, including early railways and the experience of the Blitz and blackout in Britain during the Second World War. Finally, there are lessons on the legacy of the Greeks and the achievements of the earliest civilisations: Ancient Egypt and Benin.

Stone Age farming

⊙ Lesson overview

Lesson enquiry question

How can we find out about the first farmers in the Stone Age?

Resources required

Sources:

❶ Image of Stone Age quern available from www.teachinghistory100.org/objects/neolithic_quern.

❷ Image of Stone Age sickle (you can easily source this yourself by typing 'Stone Age sickle' into a search engine).

❸ Image of Stone Age stone axe (again, you can easily source this yourself by typing 'Stone Age axe' into a search engine).

Other:

- Ingredients for baking flatbread:
  - 200g plain or wholemeal flour
  - ¼ tsp salt
  - 100ml warm water
  - 2 tbsp oil (olive, sunflower or vegetable), plus extra for cooking.

Lesson focus

Describe:

Describe how people in the early Stone Age were hunter-gatherers.

Explain:

Explain some of the ways in which the first farmers used tools to farm their crops.

Curriculum link:

Changes in Britain from the Stone Age to the Iron Age – late Neolithic hunter-gatherers and early farmers.

❶ Stone Age quern. © The Trustees of the British Museum.

    Copyright © Clare Horrie and Rachel Hillman, 2020

🚀 Starter activity

Discuss with the pupils about food and farming today. You could bring in some different types of food from the supermarket for the pupils to pass around or you could place them in a feely bag and get the pupils to identify each object by touch. Some examples might include a loaf of bread, a pint of milk, cheese, sausages, fruit and vegetables. Say that we generally buy our food in supermarkets today, but where has the produce come from? How does it reach our supermarket shelves? Talk to the pupils about the ways in which farmers grow crops and rear animals today, as well as the way in which we also export and import some of our food.

Explain to the pupils that people in the early Stone Age were called hunter-gatherers. Ask the pupils what they think this term means. Explain that this meant that people had to hunt or catch everything that they ate. They would move from place to place looking for food. You could use some simple props here like netting to represent the way in which Stone Age people would catch fish in the rivers, a sharpened stick to show how they hunted animals (explain that these were often topped with flint or bone spears), and fake animal fur to represent the way in which they used animal skin for their clothing. Emphasise how each day would be focussed on finding food for meals.

⭐ Main activity

Explain to the pupils that they are now going to look at some images of artefacts or objects from the late Stone Age (Neolithic) to find out how people began to move away from being hunter-gathers, and how they started to live in a new way. They started to clear areas of land and began to set up early farms.

Ask the pupils to work in pairs, and give them images of the different Stone Age artefacts. Explain that each artefact was used in some way for farming and that they need to study the image carefully and see if they can work out what the object is and how it was used. The first image could be worked through as a whole-class activity if helpful. Then, when the children are discussing in their pairs, you could share some questions and handy hints for each object (as described below) to help the children make their observations. Once the pupils have had a go at making their own observations, you can offer them the correct description for each object.

Image 1: Stone Age quern

Questions:

- What do you think this object is made from?
- How might it feel to hold or touch this object?
- There are two parts to this object: a smaller stone and a larger piece. What do you think they might have been used for?

Handy hint: This object would have helped to prepare an ingredient needed to make bread!

Description: This object is a quern. Early farmers grew wheat and barley, and a quern was used for grinding the crop into flour to make bread.

Image 2: Wood and flint sickle

Questions:

- What do you think this object is made from?
- How might it feel to hold or touch this object?
- How do you think this object was used?

Handy hint: This object helped farmers to harvest their crops.

Description: This object is a sickle made of wood. The wood is curved and there would have been a sharp flint at the end so that the farmers could cut the wheat in the fields. This was then ground to make flour for bread.

Image 3: Stone axe

Questions:

- What do you think this object is made from?
- How might it feel to hold or touch this object?
- What do you think this object was used for?

Handy hint: This object would have helped farmers to prepare the land for growing crops.

Description: This object is an axe made of a stone blade and wooden handle. Leather straps held the blade in place and farmers used these for cutting down trees to clear the land for farming. Axes were also a status symbol to show the importance of their owner.

Gather the pupils together and ask them to feed back their findings. Talk to the pupils further about Neolithic farmers and how they built their farms by clearing the land to create fields and houses. You could talk more about the crops that they farmed (such as flax for cloth, beans and peas) and the domesticated animals that they started to keep (such as cows, sheep and pigs). These changes paved the way for farming today.

🖊 Creative activity

Pupils could grind their own wheat to make flour and bake their own flatbread. There is a great recipe on BBC Food that is suitable to try with children, available at: www.bbc.co.uk/food/recipes/quick_flatbreads_43123.

Copyright © Clare Horrie and Rachel Hillman, 2020

Bronze Age technology

⟳ Lesson overview

Lesson enquiry question

How can we find out about the impact of technology in the Bronze Age?

Resources required

Sources:

1 Images of spear heads.

2 Image of Bronze Age gold necklace.

3 Image of Bronze Age loom (you can easily source this from the internet by typing 'Bronze Age loom' into a search engine).

Other:

- A selection of modern-day objects made of different material types.
- A selection of modern-day objects made of copper, tin and bronze.
- Copper wire.

Lesson focus

Describe:

Describe how settlers to Britain brought new skills and how the Beakers introduced metal and the advent of the Bronze Age.

Explain:

Explain some of the ways in which Bronze Age technology had an impact on people's lives.

Curriculum link:

Changes in Britain from the Stone Age to the Iron Age – Bronze Age religion, technology and travel.

1 Spear heads. © The Trustees of the British Museum.

1 Bronze Age gold necklace. © Ashmolean Museum/ Heritage Images/Getty Images.

 Copyright © Clare Horrie and Rachel Hillman, 2020

🚀 Starter activity

Bring in a selection of objects made of different types of materials, such as a wooden spoon, some pottery, a plastic cup, a metal fork or a bronze bracelet. Ask the pupils to explore the items in small groups and discuss what they're made from, what they're used for, why that material has been used for the object (think about the properties of that material), and what it feels like to touch the object.

Once the pupils have had an opportunity to explore the different materials, bring them back together to share their findings. Now see if the pupils can arrange the objects on a spectrum with the newest type of material at one end and the oldest type of material at the other end. Ask them to explain their reasoning. Do they know how each type of material is made?

Explain to the pupils that around 4,000 years ago, new groups of people came to Britain. Some of these settlers were called 'Beaker people' after the pottery cups (beakers) that they brought with them. They also knew how to make metal, a skill that transformed the lives of many people and brought Britain into the Bronze Age.

⭐ Main activity

Explain to the pupils that the Beaker people's ability to make and work with metal had a significant impact on the way in which people lived. They mined for copper and tin, which they then used to make bronze. You could bring in some examples of each of these types of metal and explain how the tin and copper were heated at high temperatures and mixed together to make bronze. The Beakers' skill as metalworkers had an impact on the tools and weapons that people could use. This, in turn, changed the way in which people lived. Explain to the pupils that they are now going to explore some of these changes by studying three images of artefacts (objects) from the Bronze Age in Britain.

Ask the pupils to work in pairs or small groups and give them images of the different Bronze Age artefacts. Explain that each artefact was made of metal and that they need to study the image carefully to see if they can work out what the object was, how it was used and then consider the impact it might have had on the way in which people lived. The first image could be worked through as a whole-class activity if helpful. You could also provide pupils with the following questions to support their examination of each object. Once the pupils have had a chance to discuss in their pairs or small groups, gather them together and ask them to feed back their findings. You can then offer them the correct description for each object.

Image 1: Bronze Age spear heads

Questions:

- What do you think these objects are?
- How might they have been used?
- Similar tools were made to use for farming. They would have been used to clear the land ready for crops. Why do you think metal tools would have been more effective than stone tools? What impact would this have had on farming at this time?

Description: These objects are Bronze Age spear heads. Once made, they would have been fitted onto wooden handles. Metal tools made it easier and quicker to clear the land to grow crops. This meant that more land could be cleared, more crops grown and more people fed.

Image 2: Bronze Age necklace

Questions:

- What do you think this object is?
- How might it have been used?
- Why do you think people started to wear metal in this way? What did objects like this tell others about the person who owned them?

Description: This object is a gold necklace from the Bronze Age. Metalworkers were able to craft metal into beautiful jewellery that was then used to demonstrate the importance of its wearer.

Image 3: Bronze Age loom

Questions:

- What do you think this object is?
- How do you think it was used?
- What impact do you think this object had on people's lives?

Description: This object is a Bronze Age loom. Metalworkers were able to craft the different shapes and parts needed for the loom. This meant that people could wear woollen clothes for the first time, helping them to keep warm and lead more comfortable lives.

To conclude the activity, lead a class discussion about the different ways in which the developments of the Bronze Age impacted on people's lives.

✏️ Creative activity

Pupils could design their own jewellery by first drawing a diagram and then crafting it from copper wire. Alternatively, pupils could investigate other examples of Bronze Age technology and compile a class fact file to share with other children in the school.

Iron Age art and culture

↻ Lesson overview

Lesson enquiry question

What do the objects reveal about life in the Iron Age?

Resources required

Sources:

❶ Iron Age shield.

❷ Iron Age reaping hook.

❸ Iron Age bowl.

Other:

- Three copies of the worksheet blown up to A3 size and laminated (if possible).
- Sticky notes.
- Air-drying clay.

Lesson focus

Describe:

Describe what the Iron Age was.

Explain:

Explain some of the ways in which Iron Age artefacts can reveal information about people's lives.

Curriculum link:

Changes in Britain from the Stone Age to the Iron Age – Iron Age hill forts: tribal kingdoms, farming, art and culture.

❶ Iron Age shield. © CM Dixon/Print Collector/Getty Images.

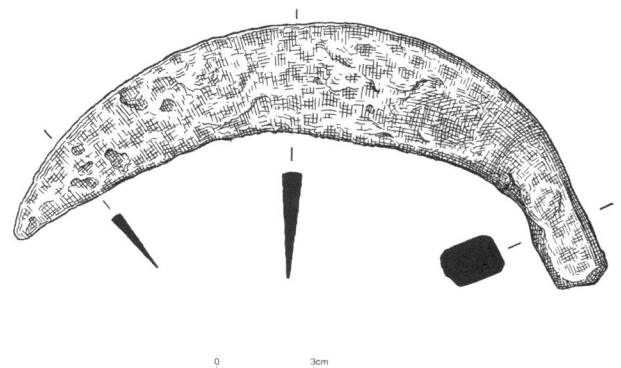

❷ Iron Age reaping hook. © The Trustees of the British Museum.

❸ Iron Age bowl. © The Trustees of the British Museum.

 Copyright © Clare Horrie and Rachel Hillman, 2020

🚀 Starter activity

Set a scenario for the pupils. Explain that they've just arrived in a new place and that they need to find the best environment to settle in. Ask them to work in small groups and to make a list of the types of things that they might need in order to survive in a particular area, such as forests for creating shelter, a source of water, a high vantage point to spot attack or threat, and so on.

Ask the pupils to share their ideas with each other. What would the 'best' settlement have?

Explain to the pupils that the Iron Age saw Celtic people spreading out across Europe and many settling in Britain. (You could use a visual map to demonstrate this movement and settlement.) People at this time lived in different clans or tribes, governed by warrior kings. They were all looking for the ideal place to settle and many rival tribes fought each other competing for the best land. They built large hill forts, surrounded by walls and ditches to protect them from attack. The Celts had also discovered iron, a material that transformed the lives of many people and brought Britain into the Iron Age.

⭐ Main activity

Explain to the pupils that the Celts' discovery and use of iron had a significant impact on the way in which they lived. Tell the pupils that they are now going to explore some images of artefacts that have survived from Iron Age Britain. Using their observation and interpretation skills, they are going to find out what these objects can tell us about people's lives at this time.

Stick the three A3 worksheets around the room and label them Image 1, 2 and 3. Ask the pupils to work in pairs or small groups, and give them images of the Iron Age artefacts (make sure these are also labelled Image 1, 2 and 3). Explain that they need to study each image carefully to see if they can work out what the object was, how it was used and what it can tell us about people's lives in the Iron Age. Ask the pupils to write their answers on sticky notes and then allow each group in turn to stick them onto the relevant A3 worksheet. In this way, the pupils can share their findings and also leave further questions for other groups to answer!

Once the pupils have had a chance to stick their findings on the worksheets, you can discuss what they've written as a class, including any further questions they may have left. You can then offer them the following descriptions for each object.

Image 1: Iron Age shield

This object is an Iron Age shield. Iron Age Britain was a very dangerous and violent place, as different clans (groups of people) fought rival tribes and competed for the best settlements. The discovery of iron meant that they could forge weapons from this strong and durable material, and were better placed to defend themselves.

Image 2: Iron Age reaping hook

This object is an Iron Age reaping hook. It would have been used as a tool for farming, attached to a long wooden pole, to reap (cut and collect) the crops. Iron was much stronger than bronze and made farming much easier than before, enabling the Celts to clear large areas of land. They even cleared forests as their numbers grew, and used these areas for crops. More and more people could be fed, and surplus food was produced and stored for the winter months. The Celts also used iron to make ploughs for farming, which meant that they could prepare large areas of land quickly and easily for planting crops.

Image 3: Iron Age bowl

This object is an Iron Age pottery bowl. Towards the end of the Iron Age, people had invented and started to use the potter's wheel. This meant that pottery was no longer made from the coil technique (coiling long pieces of clay to join together to make pots) but could be made on the wheel in different shapes and sizes. The different types of pottery and equipment that people could use to eat and drink from, and to cook with, greatly increased.

Once this activity is complete, facilitate a class discussion about what the different artefacts reveal about people's lives in the Iron Age.

✏️ Creative activity

Pupils could design and make their own clay pots, using the early Iron Age technique of coiling. To do this, pupils use a rolling pin to make a thick but flat slab of clay for the base of the pot. They then roll pieces of clay until they form long coils. They place one coil around the edge of the base and blend and smooth the joint. They then place a second coil on top of the first, again blending and smoothing the joint. They keep adding layers in this way until they have formed a pot.

Alternatively, pupils could design their own Iron Age shields using source 1 as inspiration.

Worksheet: Iron Age art and culture

What TYPE of object is it?	What was it USED for?

WHAT does the object reveal about life in the Iron Age?

What can the object tell us about people's lives in the Iron Age?	Can you think of a question about the object that you'd like the next group to answer?

Copyright © Clare Horrie and Rachel Hillman, 2020

Roman Army

⟳ Lesson overview

Lesson enquiry question

How well protected were Roman soldiers?

Resources required

Sources:

❶ Marble statue of Roman Emperor in military dress.

❷ Roman helmet.

❸ Images of additional Roman weapons sourced from the internet, including:

- Roman sword
- Roman shield
- Roman chain mail armour.

Other:

- Cards photocopied and cut out from the worksheet showing the Latin names of Roman objects. Copy enough for one per group.
- Cardboard.
- Scissors.
- Sticky tape.
- Paper.
- Colouring pencils.

Lesson focus

Describe:

Describe how a Roman soldier was dressed.

Explain:

Explain how well protected a Roman soldier was.

Curriculum link:

The Roman Empire – the impact of technology, culture and beliefs.

❶ Marble statue of Roman Emperor in military dress. © DeAgostini/Getty Images.

❷ Roman helmet. © CM Dixon/Print Collector/ Getty Images.

Copyright © Clare Horrie and Rachel Hillman, 2020

🚀 Starter activity

Introduce the image of the marble statue on the whiteboard as a mystery document. Ask the pupils to discuss in pairs what they can see. The following are suggested questions to ask or to use to guide their discussion:

- What do you think the object is made from?
- What do you think the object would be like to hold and touch? (For example, smooth, heavy and so on.)
- Describe the object. What can you see? How is the person dressed?
- What do you think their role was?
- Why do you think this object was made?

Now bring the pupils back together and encourage them to feed back their observations.

Explain to the pupils that this object shows the torso (body) of a Roman Emperor in military clothing. It was probably made as a statue to impress those who saw it. Ask the pupils to look carefully at the way the statue is dressed and ask the following questions:

- Does this look like the type of clothing that a soldier would wear today? Why or why not?
- Does this clothing offer a soldier protection?
- Why do you think it has been designed in this way?

Explain to the pupils that soldiers wore a linen under-tunic with a short woollen tunic over the top. The belt was used to alter the length of the tunic as the fabric could be pulled up and over the belt. The cloak was called a paenula and made of a felt-like fabric. The soldiers' boots were called caligae and made of leather.

Ask the pupils if they think the Roman soldiers were well protected. Why or why not?

✏️ Creative activity

Pupils could make their own Roman shields and practise Roman military drills in groups or even as a whole class! The shields can be made from cardboard and covered in paper coloured in with a Roman design. They can add cardboard handles across the back of the shields using sticky tape.

⭐ Main activity

Explain to the pupils that they are now going to look at some further images of Roman artefacts to find out more about the Roman army. Ask the pupils to work in small groups and give them the following images on A5-sized cards:

- Image 1: galea (Roman helmet)
- Image 2: gladius (Roman sword), source image from the internet
- Image 3: scutum (Roman shield), source image from the internet
- Image 4: lorica hamata (Roman chain mail armour), source image from the internet.

The pupils can then answer the following questions about each source in their groups:

- What type of object is this?
- What material is it made from?
- How would you describe it?
- What can this object tell us about the Roman army?

As a final challenge, hand each group a set of cards (printed using the worksheet on page 101) and see if the pupils can match the image of each object with its Latin name.

Once they have finished the group tasks, gather the pupils together and ask them to feed back their findings. Pose the enquiry question again: 'How well protected were Roman soldiers?' Invite comments from the pupils based on the evidence that they've seen.

Explain that Roman soldiers were very well protected and armed. Over their tunics (and not visible in the mystery document), soldiers would wear lorica hamata, which was Roman chain mail. They would also have weapons (two javelins, a sword and a dagger), and a large shield. The soldiers used different-shaped shields depending on their role in the battlefield.

Roman soldiers took part in rigorous training, including marching and weapons training. When they went into battle, the Roman soldiers often used their shields to protect them. They often stood in the testudo formation (tortoise formation). This involved the soldiers at the front and the sides interlocking their shields to form a barrier, and the soldiers in the back lines placing shields over their heads to protect the soldiers underneath. There are some good examples on YouTube of people recreating this formation, so you can show the pupils a video to bring it to life.

Only men were allowed to be Roman soldiers (and they had to be Roman citizens). However, non-Roman citizens could also fight as auxiliaries. They were not paid as much as Roman soldiers and they did not have use of the best armour and weapons.

Copyright © Clare Horrie and Rachel Hillman, 2020

Worksheet: Latin names for Roman objects

Cut up these cards showing Latin names and ask your class to match them to the images of the Roman objects.

gladius	lorica hamata
galea	scutum

Roman leisure and entertainment

⊙ Lesson overview

Lesson enquiry question

How did the Romans have fun?

Resources required

Sources:

❶ Roman board game, available at www. teachinghistory100.org/objects/roman_game_board.

❷ Roman gladiators vase, available at www. teachinghistory100.org/objects/roman_gladiators.

Lesson focus

Describe:

Describe some of the different forms of Roman entertainment.

Explain:

Explain what these types of pastimes reveal about Roman interests and culture.

Curriculum link:

The Roman Empire – the impact of technology, culture and beliefs.

❷ Roman gladiators vase.
© CM Dixon/Print Collector/ Getty Images.

Copyright © Clare Horrie and Rachel Hillman, 2020

🚀 Starter activity

Discuss with the pupils some of the different things that they do to have fun and enjoy themselves. You could make a class list of ideas or get the pupils to mime an activity or pastime in pairs for the rest of the class to guess.

Ask the pupils why we have leisure activities and pastimes. What do they help us to do? Talk about the fact that not only do we relax and have fun but we also use games to help children learn and reinforce appropriate behaviour (for example literacy skills, rules, taking turns, playing with others, and so on). In this way, the way in which people have fun can tell us a lot about the society in which they live.

Display the image of the Roman board game on the whiteboard. Ask the pupils to discuss in pairs what they can see. Suggested questions to ask or guide their discussion include:

- What do you think the object is made from?
- What do you think the object would be like to hold and touch? (For example smooth, heavy and so on.)
- Describe the object. What can you see?
- What do you think the object was used for?
- Why do you think this object was made?

Now bring the pupils back together and encourage them to feed back their observations.

Explain to the pupils that this object is on display at Llandudno Museum in Wales. It was discovered at the site of an old Roman military fort and is a Roman board game called latrunculi. The smaller stones are counters and this game is a bit like modern-day draughts (players attempt to capture their opponent's pieces). This game would have been very popular, and some Romans might have gambled as they played. Romans would play board games like this when they gathered together at the bath houses.

Explain to the pupils that the Romans enjoyed everyday pastimes like this board game, but they also enjoyed bigger and more lavish types of entertainment.

✏️ Creative activity

Pupils could make their own latrunculi boards. To do this, they make a 12 x 8 grid and two different sets of counters in contrasting colours, such as red or black. Each set will need 12 counters and one dux (a larger counter, like a 'king'). The children can design their own shapes for these. The children can then learn how to play the game. A good explanation of the rules is available at www.bead.game/games/traditional/latrunculi.

⭐ Main activity

Explain to the pupils that they are now going to look at another image of a Roman artefact to find out about a different type of Roman entertainment.

Ask the pupils to work in pairs, and give them images of the three different scenes portrayed on the Roman gladiators vase (available online). Ask the pupils to answer the following questions and to annotate the images as they work. You could break the class up into three groups and give each group one image to look at before feeding back their findings to the rest of the class.

Image 1: Two gladiators facing each other

- What can you see in the image?
- How would you describe the way the person on the left is dressed?
- How is the person on the right dressed? Does he look better protected than the figure on the left? Why or why not?
- What have the men been doing?
- Why is the man on the right raising his hand?
- These images are displayed on a particular type of object. What do you think it was used for and why were these images used?

Image 2: Two gladiators fighting a bear

- What can you see in the image?
- How would you describe the way each of the people are dressed? Why might they be dressed in this way?
- What are the men doing? Why do you think this?
- These images are displayed on a particular type of object. What do you think it was used for and why were these images used?

Image 3: The animal hunt

- What can you see in the image?
- Why are all of these animals running? What do you think is happening?
- Why would this be a type of Roman entertainment?
- These images are displayed on a particular type of object. What do you think it was used for and why were these images used?

Gather the pupils together and ask them to feed back their findings. Explain the provenance of the gladiator vase (drinking cup) and how it shows different types of combat in a Roman amphitheatre: gladiator against gladiator, gladiator against animal, and animal against animal. What does this type of entertainment tell us about the Romans and how they viewed combat and battle?

Explain how gladiators were often slaves or free men who had chosen to fight through circumstance. They were seen as the lowest in the social pecking order, and a wealthy, important person would never fight as a gladiator. The fact that Roman ampitheatres were built in parts of Britain indicates the extent to which the Romanisation of the country was taking place.

Roman gods (beliefs and culture)

↻ Lesson overview

Lesson enquiry question

What can Roman artefacts tell us about Roman beliefs?

Resources required

Sources:

❶ Stone artefact of Hercules (Herakles) wrestling with two snakes.

❷ Stone carving of Minerva from Roman temple in Bath.

Lesson focus

Describe:

Describe some of the different ways in which Romans worshipped their gods.

Explain:

Explain some of the stories about Hercules and Minerva.

Curriculum link:

The Roman Empire – the impact of technology, culture and beliefs.

❶ Stone artefact of Hercules (Herakles) wrestling with two snakes. © CM Dixon/Print Collector/Getty Images.

❷ Stone carving of Minerva from Roman temple in Bath. © Universal History Archive/Universal Images Group via Getty Images.

  Copyright © Clare Horrie and Rachel Hillman, 2020

🚀 Starter activity

Display the image of the stone artefact of Hercules on the whiteboard. Ask the pupils to discuss in pairs what they can see. Suggested questions to ask and guide their discussion include:

- What do you think the object is made from?
- What do you think the object would be like to hold and touch? (For example smooth or heavy.)
- Describe the object; what does the figure look like? Are they an adult or a child? How can you tell? What is the figure doing?
- Why do you think this object was made?

Now bring the pupils back together and encourage them to feed back their observations and inferences. Explain to the pupils that this object is on display in the British Museum and that it shows one of the Roman gods as a baby. Religion was central to everyday Roman life, and they believed in lots of different gods and goddesses. The gods had to be pleased and placated with regular offerings and sacrifices. The Romans feared the gods' anger and the terrible things that might happen if they were displeased. They built temples to worship them and told stories about them.

Tell the story of Hercules and the snakes, and explain how this image depicts what happened. You could use a story bag here with props to recount the story, or find images from the internet to support the tale. Hercules was the son of Zeus and Alkmene. Zeus was a god and Alkmene was a mortal. Zeus's divine wife Hera hated Alkmene and disliked Hercules from the moment he was born. As he lay in his cradle, she sent two snakes to attack him. Hercules strangled the snakes, one in each hand.

You could go on to tell pupils more about Hercules and his life, including the Twelve Labours of Hercules and his other adventures. Alternatively, pupils could carry out their own research into this.

Explain to the pupils that Hercules was known as Herakles in Ancient Greek beliefs and was described as the greatest of Greek heroes. The Romans adopted many of the Greek gods, often changing their names and adding detail of their own to the stories.

⭐ Main activity

Explain to the pupils that they are now going to look at another image of a Roman artefact, to find out about a different Roman god. Ask the pupils to work in pairs, and give them images of the stone pediment showing Minerva. Ask the pupils to answer the following questions and annotate the images:

- What can you see in the images?
- How would you describe the head in the centre of the image? What type of creature represents his beard?
- Can you spot the images of the owl and the helmet? What qualities do you think these might represent?
- Can you spot the Tritons (half men and half fish)? What might these tell us about this Roman god?
- Where do you think these images were displayed? What are they made from?

Gather the pupils together and ask them to feed back their findings.

Explain the provenance of the stone pediment and how it comes from a scene that would have hung at a Roman temple in Bath (the site of a healing spring). It represents the Roman goddess Minerva (she was known as Athena by the Ancient Greeks). The owl represents her wisdom and the helmet shows her military powers. She was the Roman goddess of wisdom and healing. The snake-bearded head is meant to represent the snake-haired gorgon Medusa that Minerva wore on her breastplate in battle.

You could now tell pupils the stories of Minerva's birth or her transformation of Arachne into a spider. Again, you could use props or images from the internet to help bring the story to life. Pupils could also freeze-frame one of the key scenes from these stories.

Explain that we can learn a lot about Roman beliefs and religion from these artefacts that have been left behind, before asking:

- What can't these objects reveal about Roman religion?
- How else might we find this out?

✏️ Creative activity

Pupils could design their own god. What form would their god take and what important qualities would they have?

Discovery at Sutton Hoo

⟳ Lesson overview

Lesson enquiry question

What important discovery was made at Sutton Hoo in Suffolk?

Resources required

Sources:

1 The king's great gold belt buckle.

2 Letter from an official at the Department of British Medieval Antiquities at the British Museum to the Inspector of Ancient Monuments, 8th June 1939.

Other:

• Transcript for source 2.

Lesson focus

Describe:

Describe the Sutton Hoo helmet that was found in 1939 in a burial mound in Suffolk with a vast collection of weapons, a 27-metre-long ship and many other valuable objects, such as dishes, musical instruments and coins. The discovery was so important because it tells us a lot about the Anglo-Saxons and their connections with other countries. Although the helmet belonged to a powerful war leader, we cannot be certain who was buried at Sutton Hoo.

Explain:

Explain that the discovery also changed opinions of the Anglo-Saxon period as 'the dark ages'.

Curriculum link:

Britain's settlement by Anglo-Saxons and Scots: Anglo-Saxon art and culture.

1 The king's great gold belt buckle.
© DEA PICTURE LIBRARY/De Agostini via Getty Images.

Copyright © Clare Horrie and Rachel Hillman, 2020

🚀 Starter activity

Show the class the source and explain that this object was found buried in 1939. Discuss the following:

- What is this object?
- What is it made of?
- How is it decorated?
- Can you see snakes and birds?
- What does the object tell us about the person who owned it?
- Why is it so elaborately decorated?
- What does the object tell us about Anglo-Saxon times?

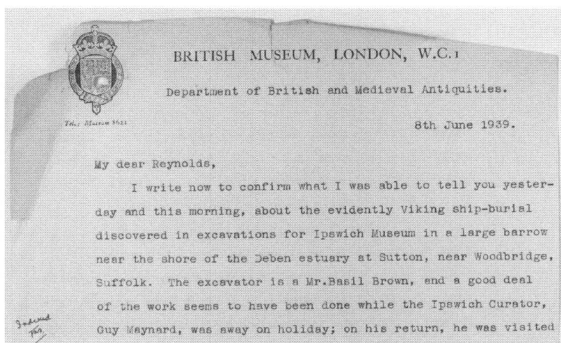

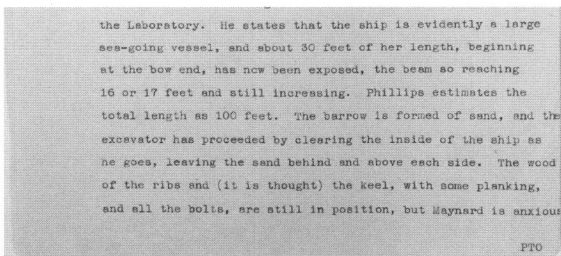

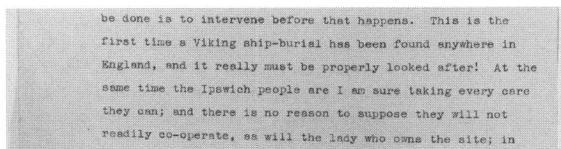

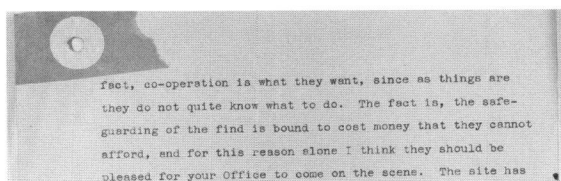

2 Letter from an official at the Department of British Medieval Antiquities at the British Museum to the Inspector of Ancient Monuments, 8th June 1939.

⭐ Main activity

Now introduce the letter from an official at the Department of British Medieval Antiquities at the British Museum to the Inspector of Ancient Monuments, 8th June 1939. Ask the pupils to think about the following questions. You can hand out the transcript on page 108 if needed.

- Where has Basil Brown discovered a ship burial?
- What museum does he work for?
- What have they found so far?
- Why do you think the British Museum was contacted?
- What are the dangers of uncovering the ship without protecting it with a shelter?

Follow this up with a feedback and plenary discussion on the pupils' findings.

Now show your class a selection of ten to 15 modern objects. Ask the class to think about what an archaeologist in 1,600 years' time might dig up and what might not have survived.

✏️ Creative activity

Print out a selection of objects from the Sutton Hoo ship burial from the British Museum website. Pupils can write their own labels saying what the objects are and what they tell us about the Anglo-Saxons.

📄 Transcript

Letter from an official at the Department of British Medieval Antiquities at the British Museum to the Inspector of Ancient Monuments, 8th June 1939

Department of British and Medieval Antiquities.
8th June 1939.

My dear Reynolds,

I write now to confirm what I was able to tell you yesterday and this morning, about the evidently Viking ship-burial discovered in excavations for Ipswich Museum in a large barrow near the shore of the Deben estuary at Sutton, near Woodbridge, Suffolk. The excavator is a Mr. Basil Brown, and a good deal of the work seems to have been done while the Ipswich Curator, Guy Maynard, was away on holiday;

…

He states that the ship is evidently a large sea-going vessel, and about 30 feet of her length, beginning at the bow end, has now been exposed, the beam so reaching 16 or 17 feet and still increasing. Phillips estimates the total length as 100 feet. The barrow is formed of sand, and the excavator has proceeded by clearing the inside of the ship as he goes, leaving the sand behind and above each side. The wood of the ribs and (it is thought) the keel, with some planking, and all the bolts, are still in position, but Maynard is anxious

about erosion by wind, and one may add that if the sun and wind action now going on is followed by rain, the exposed portion may be irretrievably ruined. I put the position to Dr. Plenderleith, our Laboratory chief, this morning, and he had no hesitation in urging that the exposed portion should be covered up again at once, and the digging suspended until a shelter can be built over the whole barrow.

…

This is the first time a Viking ship-burial has been found anywhere in England, and it really must be properly looked after! At the same time the Ipswich people are I am sure taking every care they can; and there is no reason to suppose they will not readily co-operate, as will the lady who owns the site; in

fact, co-operation is what they want, since as things are they do not quite know what to do. The fact is, the safe-guarding of the find is bound to cost money that they cannot afford, and for this reason alone I think they should be pleased for your Office to come on the scene.

Copyright © Clare Horrie and Rachel Hillman, 2020

Anglo-Saxon art: The Fuller Brooch

⟳ Lesson overview

Lesson enquiry question

How can we find out about Anglo-Saxon art?

Resources required

Source:

❶ The Fuller Brooch, late ninth century.

Other:

- Worksheet: Design your own brooch. Photocopy one per pupil.

Lesson focus

Describe:

Describe how we can discover more about art and ideas in Anglo-Saxon times with this brooch.

Explain:

Explain that this brooch is made of hammered silver inlaid with a black material called niello.

Curriculum link:

Britain's settlement by Anglo-Saxons and Scots: Anglo-Saxon art and culture.

🚀 Starter activity

Show the class modern-day pictures of people wearing jewellery and ask them if any of them wear jewellery. Discuss the following with the pupils and record their ideas:

- Why do people wear jewellery?
- What sort of jewellery do they wear?
- How could historians find out about jewellery in the time of the Anglo-Saxons?
- Why could this be difficult?

✏️ Creative activity

Pupils could design their own version of the Fuller Brooch with images that are important to them. Use the worksheet on page 110 to support this activity.

❶ The Fuller Brooch, late ninth century. © The Trustees of the British Museum.

⭐ Main activity

Give the class copies of the source image and ask them to work in pairs or small groups. Tell them that this object is 114 mm (4.5 inches) across. It is called the Fuller Brooch after the person who owned it and gave it to the British Museum. It was once considered a fake because it was in such good condition!

They will need to look carefully at the image and discuss:

- What can you see in the image?
- What is shown in the border and the inner circle?
- What metal is it made of?
- What effect in the brooch does the black material make? (The images stand out.)
- Who do you think owned this brooch?
- Why do you think people wore brooches in Anglo-Saxon times?
- Does the brooch give a message?
- Does the shape help with its message in any way?
- What does the brooch tell us about the Anglo-Saxons.

The following information about the brooch will help you to support the pupils' discussions. Guide the pupils towards this information through their observations and interpretations. The five figures represent the senses. The centre is Sight with the large eyes; Taste has a hand in his mouth; Smell has his hands behind his back and is standing between two tall plants; Touch has his hands together; Hearing has his hand on his ear. The border has patterns that show humans, plants and birds, perhaps to represent man's position in the created order.

✎ Worksheet: Design your own brooch

Design your own version of the Fuller Brooch. Think about what you want to include on your brooch and why.

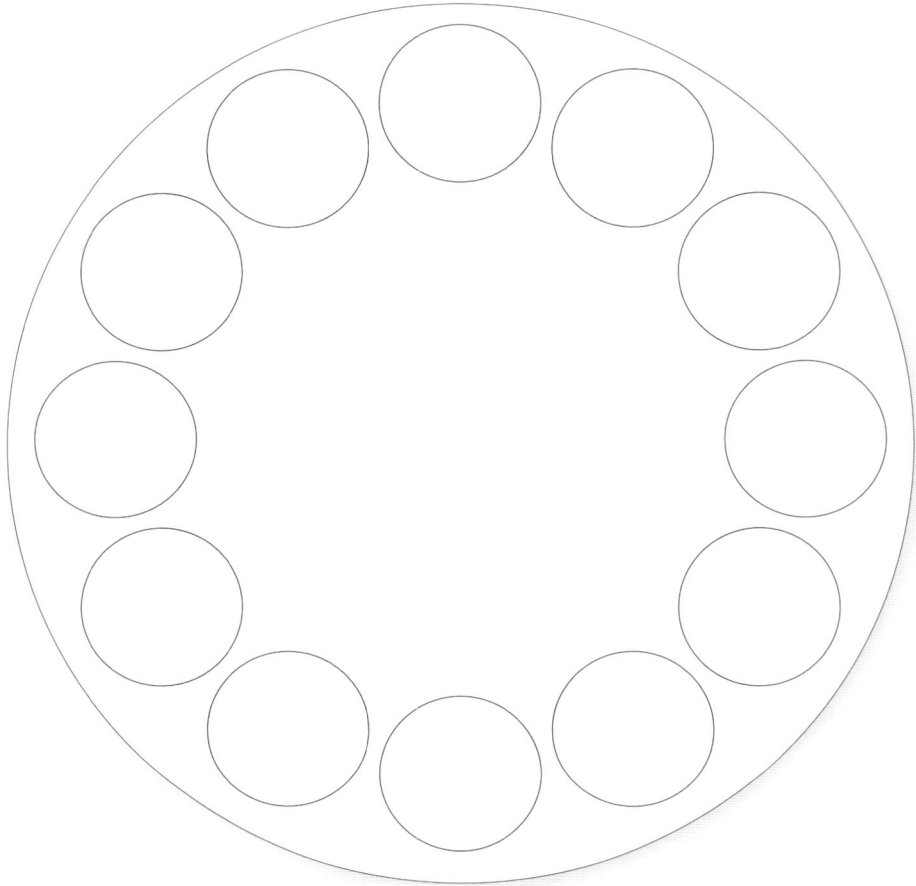

What have you included on your brooch? Why are these things important to you?

_____

_____

_____

_____

_____

_____

_____

   Copyright © Clare Horrie and Rachel Hillman, 2020

Anglo-Saxon art: Writing tablet

⟳ Lesson overview

Lesson enquiry question

What can we find out about Anglo-Saxon learning?

Resources required

Source:

❶ Blythburgh writing tablet.

Other:

• Colouring pencils.

Lesson focus

Describe:

Describe what this object can reveal about Anglo-Saxon writing.

Explain:

Explain that parchment, a thin material made from the prepared skin of an animal, usually a sheep or goat, was used to write on in Anglo-Saxon times. It was expensive and took time to make. This object was a way around that.

Curriculum link:

Britain's settlement by Anglo-Saxons and Scots: Anglo-Saxon art and culture.

❶ Blythburgh writing tablet. © The Trustees of the British Museum.

🚀 Starter activity

Ask the pupils to make a list of all the different ways we record language. They can do this individually or in pairs. Then find out who has the most suggestions and share the results.

After this initial activity, ask the pupils to think about why it would be more difficult for the Anglo-Saxons to record language.

✏️ Creative activity

As a class, research some examples of Anglo-Saxon manuscripts. The pupils can then draw and colour their own decorated letters using the initials of their own name. They could also include a decorated border on the paper. Display the pupils' work.

⭐ Main activity

Give the class copies of the source image and ask them to work in pairs or small groups. They will need to look carefully and discuss the following questions.

- What can you see in the image?
- What could the object be made of?
- What might the holes be used for?

Ask the class to share their ideas.

Now tell the pupils that the object is part of a writing tablet made of whale bone and ask:

- Can you explain how it was used?
- What does the tablet tell us about the Anglo-Saxons?
- What makes this object similar or different to a Victorian school slate?

The following information about the writing tablet will help you to support the pupils in their discussions. Guide the pupils towards this information through their observations and interpretations of the image, rather than telling it to them directly. This front panel would have been held together to a back panel by leather ties. Both panels were made of whale bone; similar objects, used by the Romans, were made of wood. On the front panel is a four-part knot design in a square frame. The back panel, which originally contained reusable wax, has traces of runic lettering. A metal 'pen' called a stylus was used to write in the wax. Sometimes the writer pressed so hard that it marked the whalebone underneath the wax, so that's probably why the runes appear on the object. The tablets were used for learning to write, drafting manuscripts or taking notes.

Runes are an alphabet used when the Anglo-Saxons came to Britain. The letters had lots of straight lines, which made it easier to carve them onto wood, stone or metal. When the Anglo-Saxons became Christians, they began using the Latin alphabet.

Copyright © Clare Horrie and Rachel Hillman, 2020

King Alfred: Was he so great?

⟳ Lesson overview

Lesson enquiry question

Was King Alfred all that great?

Resources required

Sources:

1 A drawing of King Alfred, 1733.

2 Silver penny showing Alfred the Great.

Other:

- Selection of school history books on the history of Britain and topic books on Anglo-Saxons or King Alfred.
- This article from *History Today* might help give you some context ahead of the lesson (this is for teacher reference and does not need to be shared with pupils): www.historytoday.com/archive/alfred-great-most-perfect-man-history.

Lesson focus

Describe:

Describe what these sources reveal about Alfred.

Explain:

Explain that Alfred (849–899 AD) became king in 871 AD after the death of his elder brother. He is one of many Anglo-Saxon kings, but the only one to be called 'Great' in British history. He defeated the Vikings at the Battle of Edington in 878. He was interested in learning and he tried to rule fairly. He wanted people to read and had books translated from Latin into English. He protected his kingdom of Wessex (871 to c. 886) by building forts and walled towns. He built ships to protect the coast from attack. Alfred was buried in Winchester. By the end of his reign, his coins referred to him as 'King of the English' (c. 886 to 899).

Curriculum link:

The Viking and Anglo-Saxon struggle for the Kingdom of England to the time of Edward the Confessor: Resistance by Alfred the Great.

1 A drawing of King Alfred, 1733. © The Print Collector via Getty Images.

2 Silver penny showing Alfred the Great. © Museum of London/Heritage Images/Getty Images.

🚀 Starter activity

Ask the class to make a list of qualities that would make a 'Great' king in Anglo-Saxon times. They can work on this as individuals or in pairs, before sharing and discussing the results as a class.

Now show the pupils source 1 and explain that it is a portrait of 'King Alfred the Great' drawn in 1733 by artist George Vertue. In pairs or small groups ask the pupils to discuss the following questions:

• What is this source?
• How does King Alfred's face appear in the portrait?
• How does his clothing appear in the portrait?
• Look at the various objects in the picture. What type of impression do they give of King Alfred? Why are they included?
• What do you think the scenes in the picture refer to? Why are they included?
• Does it make a difference that this is a secondary source (i.e. not from the time of King Alfred)? Discuss why or why not.
• Where do you think this image might appear?

Bring the pupils back together to discuss their findings. The following notes about the source will help you facilitate and guide the discussion. The source shows a portrait of 'King Alfred the Great' in an oval frame inscribed 'Alfredus Magnus Rex Angliae' (Alfred the Great, King of England). The King has a long beard. He wears a crown over long, curly hair and wears an ermine-lined cloak. On the table below are a crown, books, arrows, a lyre and a raven banner (a Viking battle symbol possibly meaning ability to overcome). There are also papers and geometry instruments, with scenes of battle and tents in a military encampment surrounding the portrait.

Now explore with the pupils whether this image of King Alfred is deserved or idealised. Choose some extracts about King Alfred from the class and topic books. For each text, ask pupils to compare how King Alfred is described in terms of character, appearance and achievements. Do these books match up in any way to Alfred's portrayal in the historical source?

⭐ Main activity

Explain to the pupils that they are now going to look at a primary source (source 2), a silver penny from the early 880s. Ask them to work in pairs or small groups to discuss the questions.

• Describe King Alfred on the coin, including his face and clothing.
• Who does he look like? (A Roman emperor.)
• Why has Alfred been shown like this?

• What are the differences between this and the portrait (source 1)?
• Can you work out the inscriptions on both coins? (ÆLFR / EDREX ('King Alfred') and, on the reverse, LVNDONIA (monogram for 'London').)
• Can you suggest why London appears on the reverse of the coin? (It commemorates Alfred's control of London and shows where the coin was minted.)
• What could the coin have meant to the people of London? (London would start to trade again and become important.)
• Does this source help to explain how Alfred got this reputation for 'Great'?
• Do we need more evidence?

Bring the pupils back together to discuss their findings. The following notes about the source will help you facilitate and guide the discussion.

Alfred, by the end of his reign, had increased the number of royal mints from two to nine. He also increased the silver content of coins. A coinage with his image showed his power and control over the kingdom, as he gave permission for the coins to be minted. He also wanted to increase trade and prosperity. It was very unusual for coins to name the place in which they were made. This coin is significant, as it celebrates Alfred's control of Mercia and London after the fall of the last Mercian king, Ceolwulf II (874–879). It is a way to show Alfred's authority over London, which he later rebuilt in parts.

🖊 Creative activity

Pupils make a booklet or poster showing how King Alfred has been commemorated in history, using the following examples and any others you might come across. All these examples can be found easily on Google Images.

• The Alfred Plaque: A plaque in the City of London recording the restoration of the Roman walled city by Alfred.
• Statue of Alfred the Great in Winchester: Erected in 1899, this statue marks 1,000 years since Alfred's death.
• King Alfred's Tower: in Brewham, Somerset, this tower is also known as The Folly of King Alfred the Great.
• Statue of King Alfred in Wantage, Oxfordshire, his birthplace: The statue was made in 1877 by Count Gleichen.

Copyright © Clare Horrie and Rachel Hillman, 2020

Edward the Confessor

⟳ Lesson overview

Lesson enquiry question

How far can we use images in the Abbreviato to tell us about the life of Edward the Confessor?

Resources required

Sources (all taken from the Abbreviato):

❶ Image of King Edward challenging Earl Godwin.

❷ Image of King Edward giving a ring to St John the Evangelist.

❸ Image of King Edward's vision of the Danish king drowning.

Other:

- A bag of mystery objects, such as a crown, some jewels or gems, a wooden cross, an image of Westminster Abbey, a map showing medieval Normandy and an image of Edward the Confessor's shrine. (The images can easily be sourced from the internet.)
- Question cards. Copy and cut out enough for one per pair or group.

Lesson focus

Describe:

Describe who Edward the Confessor was.

Explain:

Explain why the Abbreviato has been illustrated with stories of King Edward's 'miracles'.

Curriculum link:

The Viking and Anglo-Saxon struggle for the Kingdom of England to the time of Edward the Confessor: Edward the Confessor and his death in 1066.

❶ Image of King Edward challenging Earl Godwin.

❷ Image of King Edward giving a ring to St John the Evangelist.

❸ Image of King Edward's vision of the Danish king drowning.

Copyright © Clare Horrie and Rachel Hillman, 2020

🚀 Starter activity

Explain to the pupils that they are going to find out about a mystery person from medieval times. Use the bag of mystery objects described in the lesson overview to help the pupils start to think about who this person was. Ask the pupils to spend a few minutes exploring the different objects and images, and ask them to see if they can come up with suggestions for answers to the following questions:

- Who was this person? What job or position did they hold?
- Is there anything in the bag that tells you about the types of things that this person believed in?
- Are there any questions that you would like to ask about the images or objects and how they relate to this mystery person?

Ask the pupils to share their ideas as a class, and then explain that the mystery person they've been investigating was called Edward the Confessor. He was king of England from 1042 to 1066. You could identify this time period on the class timeline with the pupils. Discuss with the pupils what they think the name Edward the Confessor means. What does this tell us about the type of person that he was?

Explain to the pupils the relevance of the different objects and images in the mystery bag. You can use the following information to help:

- Crown, jewels and gems: To show his status as king of England.
- Wooden cross: To represent the fact that he was very religious and spent a lot of time confessing his sins to God.
- Westminster Abbey: Edward the Confessor oversaw the plans and building of Westminster Abbey from 1052 to 1065 (although the present Westminster Abbey was constructed by Henry III with most of Edward's original structure destroyed).
- Shrine: As Henry III held Edward the Confessor in such high regard, he had a new shrine built for him in Westminster Abbey and many made pilgrimages to visit the shrine.
- Map of Normandy: Edward the Confessor spent many years in exile in Normandy after being driven from England by the Danes, before returning and becoming king in 1042.

⭐ Main activity

Explain to the pupils that they are now going to find out more about Edward the Confessor from a document called the Domesday Abbreviato. This was a shortened version of a very important book called the Domesday Book. It was used by the Exchequer (the king or government's department that deals with money taken from taxation), as it contained information on who held land and could therefore be used to calculate the tax owed.

The Abbreviato was made after the Domesday Book and after the life of Edward the Confessor, around 1241, during the reign of King Henry III. King Henry admired Edward the Confessor and was a believer in the cult of Edward the Confessor (he had been made a saint in 1161). Many miracles were said to have taken place at Edward's tomb, and people also wrote about miracles that he supposedly performed during his life. King Henry III had this illustrated copy of the Abbreviato made during his reign, showing us how he believed in the cult of Edward the Confessor.

Explain to the pupils that they are going to work with copies of images from the Abbreviato that show Edward the Confessor and some of the miracles that are said to have taken place during his lifetime. The pupils will see if they can work out what each miracle was and consider how far it can tell us something about Edward the Confessor and his life.

Ask the pupils to work in pairs or small groups, and give them copies of the different images labelled 1, 2 and 3 as listed below. Ask them to work through the following questions for each image. You can use the worksheet on page 118 to create question cards to hand out to each group. Once the pupils have discussed in their pairs or groups, gather the pupils together and ask them to feed back their findings. The descriptions below will help you facilitate and guide the class discussion and answer any questions.

Image 1: King Edward challenges Earl Godwin

Questions:

- Describe what you can see in the image.
- Where do you think the people are and what are they doing?
- Why do you think King Edward the Confessor is pointing at the man wearing the green cloak?
- Do you think the King is happy with this man? Why or why not?

Description:

This image shows Edward the Confessor during a banquet at Windsor, pointing accusingly at a man called Earl Godwin. He has just become king. Years earlier, Edward's brother Alfred had travelled to England from

Copyright © Clare Horrie and Rachel Hillman, 2020

Normandy and was captured. Earl Godwin took Alfred to Harold Harefoot and he was tortured and died. During this banquet, Edward the Confessor is accusing Earl Godwin of his brother's murder. Earl Godwin claims that he is innocent and that if he were guilty the piece of bread he was eating would choke him. He then chokes on the bread and dies! In this image you can see Earl Godwin preparing to eat the bread.

Image 2: King Edward gives a ring to St John the Evangelist

Questions:

- Describe what you can see in the image.
- What do you think Edward the Confessor is giving to the other man? Why is he doing this?
- Does the man look wealthy or poor? Why do you think this?

Description:

This image shows Edward the Confessor travelling on the feast day of St John the Evangelist (one of Jesus's apostles or chief disciples). He meets a beggar on the journey and, as he has no money to give him, the King gives him a ring from his finger. Some months later, two pilgrims in Jerusalem meet the old man, who asks them to return the ring to the King. He says that he is St John the Evangelist and that the King would soon come to be with him. Not long afterwards, King Edward the Confessor dies.

Image 3: King Edward has a vision of the Danish king drowning

Questions:

- Describe what you can see in the image.
- Who are the men in the boats and what job or role do they have? How can you tell?
- Why is one of the men in the water?
- Do you think that the man in the water is an important person? Why or why not?

Description:

This image shows a vision that King Edward was supposed to have had. During a court session, Edward the Confessor is said to have explained that he'd had a vision of the king of Denmark drowning on a sea voyage to invade England. The story then says that messengers sent to England to find out what had happened said that the story was true and the king of Denmark was dead. In reality, King Svein of Denmark actually died after Edward the Confessor.

Once you've discussed each individual image in turn, ask the pupils what the different images reveal about some of the miracles that were supposed to have happened during Edward the Confessor's life. Can we believe them? Did these things really happen when Edward was king?

Explain to the pupils that these images and miracle stories are a bit like propaganda – they portray a particular image of Edward the Confessor, but we cannot take them as fact or accurate representations of Edward's life as king.

So, what do the images help us to understand about King Edward the Confessor? What they do reveal is the strength of Edward's legacy and reputation years after his death. Henry III was very keen to tell everyone about Edward's role as a saint and these images help to support this idea. The one story that is known to be partially true is the death of Earl Godwin, although whether he died by choking or a sudden illness (likely to have been a stroke) is unclear and much debated!

⏺ Creative activity

The pupils could choose a miracle to illustrate or find out about some of the other miracles from Edward the Confessor's reign.

📝 Question cards: Three miracles during Edward the Confessor's life

Image 1

Describe what you can see in the image.

Where do you think the people are and what are they doing?

Why do you think King Edward the Confessor is pointing at the man wearing the green cloak?

Do you think the King is happy with this man?

Why or why not?

Image 2

Describe what you can see in the image.

What do you think Edward the Confessor is giving to the other man? Why is he doing this?

Does the man look wealthy or poor? Why do you think this?

Image 3

Describe what you can see in the image.

Who are the men in the boats and what job or role do they have? How can you tell?

Why is one of the men in the water?

Do you think that the man in the water is an important person? Why or why not?

Copyright © Clare Horrie and Rachel Hillman, 2020

King John and Magna Carta

⊙ Lesson overview

Lesson enquiry question

Why did King John face rebellion?

Resources required

Sources:

❶ Roger de Quincy's seal.

❷ Orders from King John, May 1214.

❸ Extract from the pipe roll of King John.

Other:

• Simplified transcripts for sources 2 and 3.

Lesson focus

Describe:

Describe who King John was.

Explain:

Explain why King John faced rebellion and why the Magna Carta was issued.

Curriculum link:

A study of an aspect or theme in British history that extends pupils' chronological knowledge beyond 1066; the changing power of monarchs, using case studies such as John, Anne and Victoria.

❶ Roger de Quincy's seal. Property of Her Majesty the Queen in Right of Her Duchy of Lancaster.

🚀 Starter activity

Display the images of Roger de Quincy's seal on the whiteboard. Ask the pupils to spend a couple of minutes looking at the seal in pairs, thinking about the following questions.

- What can you see? Look very carefully and describe the images.
- What type of document do you think this was?
- What do you think it was used for?

Ask the pupils to share their ideas as a class and annotate the images on the whiteboard as they feed back their findings and suggestions. Explain to the pupils that this document is a seal and that it was used as a 'picture-signature'. Written signatures were easy to forge, so important documents were issued with a wax seal. This proved that the document was genuine, and it also showed how the owner of the seal wished to be perceived. Imagery used on the seal held particular meaning and conveyed a message to those who received it.

Ask the pupils to return to the images that Roger de Quincy has used on his seal. Why did he choose these images? What was he telling people about himself and his family? Who is the lion supposed to represent? Who is the knight supposed to be?

Explain that Roger de Quincy was a baron in the 13th century, and that he is represented by the image of the knight on the seal. The lion is supposed to represent the King. The seal is saying that Roger de Quincy is not scared of the King and that he is prepared to stand up to him. This is because Roger de Quincy's father had been one of the barons who had opposed King John in 1215. Roger is warning the Crown that he too will oppose the monarch if required.

Ask the pupils if they've heard of King John before. Why would Roger de Quincy's father and other barons at the time have needed to oppose him? You could find opposing images or contemporary film representations of King John here, sourced from the internet. Medieval monks described him as Evil King John, whereas many historians today argue that he was an energetic king who was trying to improve his situation in difficult circumstances.

Explain that King John was the younger brother of Richard the Lionheart, who had been a popular and brave king. He had spent a lot of money on the Crusades, so by the time that King John inherited the throne, the treasury was empty. As King Richard I had also been away from his country for many years, arguably the barons had become too powerful in his absence.

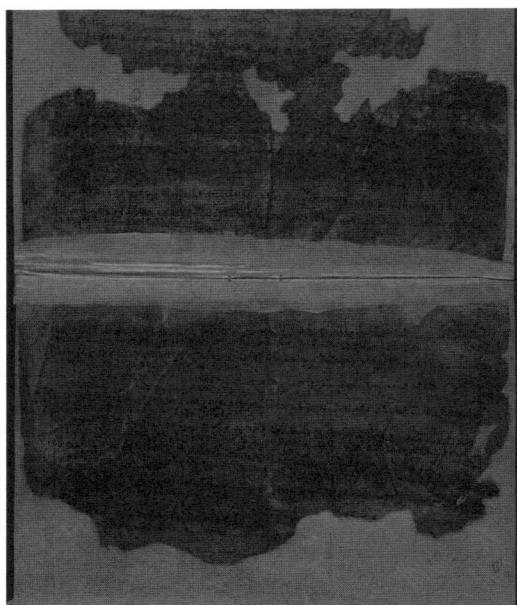

❷ Orders from King John, May 1214.

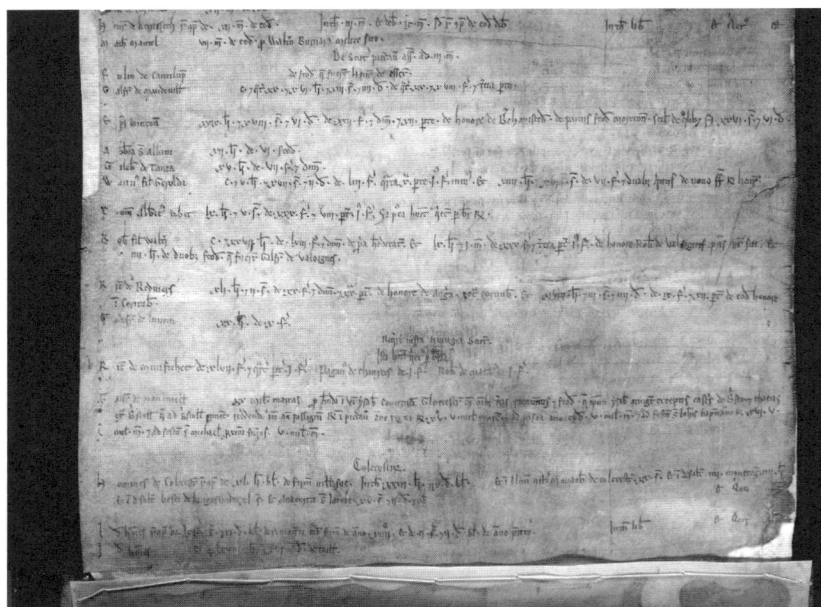

❸ Extract from the pipe roll of King John.

Copyright © Clare Horrie and Rachel Hillman, 2020

⭐ Main activity

Explain to the pupils that they are going to work with copies of original documents (sources 2 and 3) to find out why the barons were so upset with King John by 1215. Ask the pupils to work in pairs or small groups, and give them copies of the two documents with the simplified transcripts, numbered as follows. Ask them to work through the following questions. Once the pupils have discussed each document, gather them together and ask them to feed back their findings. The description of each document below will help you guide the conversation and answer any questions.

Document 1: Orders from King John, May 1214

Questions:

- What type of document is this?
- Who sent it?
- When was it sent?
- What is the King doing with the barons' lands? Why is he doing this?

Description:

This document is an order sent from King John to the rebel barons. He is confiscating their lands and giving them to his son, Henry. He is attempting to punish them and also demonstrate his power over them.

Document 2: Extract from the pipe rolls of King John

Questions:

- What type of document is this?
- What does Geoffrey de Mandeville want to do?
- What has the King told de Mandeville that he must do?
- Why has the King told Mandeville that he must do this?

Description:

This document is taken from the pipe rolls during King John's reign (these are records of money paid to and from the King). Geoffrey de Mandeville wants to marry Isabel Countess of Gloucester. If he does this, he stands to gain a lot of land and wealth from his new wife. When barons married, they were used to paying the King a tax, but in this case, King John is charging a huge amount in tax for de Mandeville's marriage. King John doesn't want de Mandeville to become a powerful threat and he also needs money.

Once you've discussed each individual source as a class, ask the pupils what the different documents reveal about King John's decisions and why the barons were upset. Explain to the pupils that when King John came to the throne, he continued to increase taxes (to protect the land that England held in France), and he eventually raised taxes and demanded even more men for fighting without asking the barons first. This was against the law. King John also upset the Church by arguing with the Pope, which meant that he was temporarily excommunicated and that all church services were banned for a number of years, which upset King John's subjects. The Church was a very important part of their daily lives.

In 1215, the Magna Carta was sealed in Runnymede, Surrey. It was a list of 63 promises between the King and his subjects, which meant that the King could not just do as he pleased but had to govern within the law. King John claimed that he had been forced into sealing the charter, but important elements endured and were referred to under later monarchs. It even influenced Bills of Rights in both the UK and the USA.

✏ Creative activity

Investigate some of the key points of the Magna Carta with the pupils. They could then write their own version of the Magna Carta for today's world and design their own seal to authenticate the document.

Examples of important key points within the 1215 Magna Carta are:

- The Church will be free from interference.
- No free man can be seized or imprisoned, or stripped of his rights or possessions... except by the lawful judgement of his peers.
- Only the normal amounts of money can be collected in taxes to run the government, unless the King's feudal tenants give their consent for more to be taken.

▤ Simplified transcript

Orders from King John, May 1214

The King sends greetings to the Sheriff of Devon. We have granted to our faithful son, Earl Henry, all the lands which previously belonged to William de Mandeville.

The King sends greetings to the Sheriff of Cornwall. We have given to Henry, our son, all the lands which previously belonged to Robert FitzWalter. We order you to give full possession of these lands to Earl Henry without delay.

The King sends greetings to Geoffrey de Marteny. We order that as soon as you have seen these letters, you take into our hands all the lands of Henry de Braybrook, destroying his houses, and taking his material wealth.

Extract from the pipe roll of King John

Geoffrey de Mandeville is to pay the King 20,000 marks to marry Isabel, Countess of Gloucester. He is to pay this amount as by marrying Isabel, he will become owner of her vast lands and wealth.

Copyright © Clare Horrie and Rachel Hillman, 2020

Queen Anne's inbox

⟳ Lesson overview

Lesson enquiry question

What's in Queen Anne's 'inbox'?

Resources required

Source:

❶ Petition from Captain James Moodie to Queen Anne.

Other:

- Simplified transcript for source 1.
- Painting supplies.

Lesson focus

Describe:

Describe this lesson's source: a petition sent to Queen Anne in the early 18th century. She received all kinds of petitions, including appeals from people against being sent to prison, petitions concerning religious practice, sale of goods or markets, requests for positions in the government or the Navy, and so on.

Explain:

Explain that this petition can reveal how a monarch was expected to rule and Anne's role as queen.

Curriculum link:

The changing power of monarchs.

🚀 Starter activity

Ask your pupils for examples of how we communicate with other people, including all types of social media, email, letters, phone, television, newspapers or magazines. Communication can also be personal and impersonal. Explain that it was different in the reign of Queen Anne, who was queen of Great Britain between 1702 and 1714. Can the pupils think why?

✏ Creative activity

The pupils have been selected by Queen Anne to paint her portrait! Using images from Google, ask them to each paint a portrait of Queen Anne.

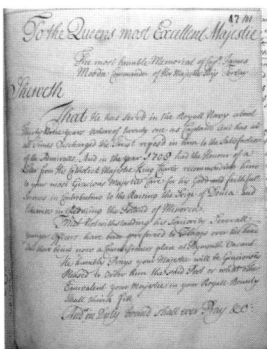

❶ Petition from Captain James Moodie to Queen Anne.

★ Main activity

Reveal the petition from Captain James Moodie to Queen Anne. Say it is a petition and define the term. What do the pupils think of the handwriting? Is it hard to read? Why? Now use the simplified transcript if needed and read the petition together as a class. Ask the pupils the following questions to explore the source:

- Who is the petition from?
- Who is it addressed to?
- How long has the writer served in the Navy?
- Why did King Charles suggest Moodie should serve Queen Anne?
- Why is Moodie writing?
- What does the petition show about the Queen's job? (She was expected to award people jobs, know about the Navy, give her opinion and deal with paperwork.)
- What do pupils think about the writing style? Is it complicated, wordy or easy to read? Is it formal or friendly?
- Why does he use capital letters for some of his words?
- Do we write like this today? Why or why not?

Now ask the pupils to imagine they are an artist who is petitioning Queen Anne to paint her portrait. Ask them to work individually to write their petition to Queen Anne and explain why they would be a good choice.

📄 Simplified transcript

Petition from Captain James Moodie to Queen Anne

To her Majesty the Queen

A humble statement of the facts from Captain James Moodie, Commander of her Majesty's ship called the Torbay.

This petition says

He has been in the Navy for 39 years, and for 21 of those years has been a captain. He has always been trusted by his bosses, the admirals in command of the ships in the navy. In 1708 he was sent a letter by the Catholic King Charles*. The letter suggested that he should work for the Queen because he had done so well in the war with Spain.

To make matters worse, even though he is so experienced in the Navy, other younger men have been given more important jobs. Now there is a job in Plymouth that needs to be filled which he could do. He begs that the Queen will be kind enough to give him the job or something else like it.

He will always pray for her.

*King Charles was the ruler of a group of countries in Europe called the Holy Roman Empire and he wanted the Spanish throne and went to war with France over it.

Copyright © Clare Horrie and Rachel Hillman, 2020

Crime and punishment

⊙ Lesson overview

Lesson enquiry question

What do the documents reveal about changes in types of punishment from the Anglo-Saxons to the Victorians?

Resources required

Sources:

❶ Image of Henry Munday and prison record.

❷ Trial by ordeal.

❸ Trial by battle.

❹ Tyburn's Triple Tree.

❺ Victorian Separate System (exercise)

❻ Table of drops.

Other:

- Simplified transcript for source 1.
- Transcript for source 5.

Lesson focus

Describe:

Describe the different types of punishments highlighted in the documents.

Explain:

Explain how punishments have changed over time and why.

Curriculum link:

Aspect or theme in British history that extends pupils' chronological knowledge beyond 1066: changes in crime and punishment from the Anglo-Saxons to the present.

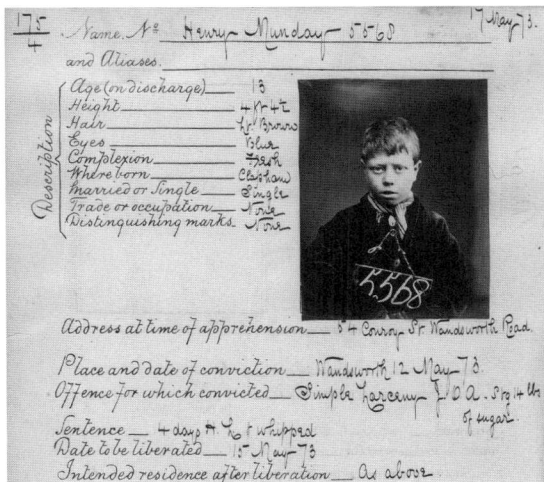

❶ Image of Henry Munday and prison record.

❷ Trial by ordeal. © Universal History Archive/Universal Images Group via Getty Images.

❸ Trial by battle.

Starter activity

Display the image of Henry Munday on the whiteboard (without any of the surrounding text). Take the mystery document approach and ask the pupils the following questions:

- What can you see?
- How old do you think this boy is?
- Do you think he is rich or poor? Why?
- Where do you think he is?
- Why do you think his photograph has been taken?
- When do you think this photograph was taken?

Encourage the pupils to feed back their answers and accept all answers as plausible at this stage. Now explain that you are going to give them the whole document that this photo comes from. Ask them to work in pairs to try to answer the following questions, using the simplified transcript if necessary:

- Can you work out what the little boy's name is?
- How old is he?
- What type of document is this?

- What has Henry done and what punishment has he been given?
- Why do you think Henry has committed this crime?

Explain to the pupils that this document comes from a Victorian prison register. Ask them what we can start to infer about crime and punishment in Victorian times from this particular record. We can see, for example, that children are sent to prison, prisoners can be whipped or given hard labour for their crimes and life was hard for those who were poor with larceny (stealing) a common crime.

Explain that crimes and the way in which we enforce law and order, and punish crimes, can vary over time. Ask the pupils to think about crimes in the UK today. What types of crime might people commit? Scribe their ideas on the whiteboard. Using a different-coloured pen, ask the pupils to think about the different types of punishments that are used as consequences for these crimes. What are the purposes of these punishments?

You could discuss with pupils the process that takes place today, from the police investigating a crime and making an arrest, through to trial in a court of law with a judge and jury.

4 Tyburn's Triple Tree.

6 Table of drops.

5 Victorian Separate System (exercise).
© Hulton Archive/Getty Images.

Copyright © Clare Horrie and Rachel Hillman, 2020

⭐ Main activity

Explain that in this lesson, the pupils are going to be looking at different documents related to punishment in the past. Each document will come from a specific time period, and pupils will consider how punishments have changed over time. What are the similarities and differences?

Ask the pupils to work in pairs, looking at each document and answering these two questions:

• What can you see in the document?
• What does this tell us about punishment at this time?

Gather the pupils together and ask them to feed back their findings. The information below will help you lead a class discussion about each source.

Document 1: Trial by ordeal, Anglo-Saxon

Trial by ordeal was seen as proof of God's judgement. Trial by hot iron or by water were common punishments. If the accused survived the ordeal, this was evidence of their innocence.

Document 2: Trial by battle, c. 1300

Trial by battle was introduced into England by the Normans after 1066. It was used to settle accusations and disagreements in the absence of a witness. If the defendant could battle from sunset to sunrise and survive, or defeat his opponent, he would go free. If the defendant was defeated and still alive, he would be hanged on the spot. In this document, from 1249, Walter Blowberme (on the left) had accused Hamo Stare (on the right) of a crime. Hamo Stare claimed the right of proving his innocence by trial by battle. However, he lost and was hanged. You can see the image of him on the gallows to the left of the image.

Document 3: Tyburn, c. 1680

This document shows the famous 'Triple Tree' at Tyburn, which was set up in 1571 (where Marble Arch now stands). Prisoners would be taken in a three-mile cart ride from Newgate Prison to Tyburn, with crowds gathering and following behind.

Document 4: Separate System, c. 1830s

This document shows the Separate System in action through the prisoners' 'daily exercise regime'. At this time, prisons were at the heart of the punishment system. Many prisons used the concept of the 'Separate System' to punish criminals through continuous solitary confinement. This meant that when they were exercising, prisoners had their faces and eyes covered so they couldn't see anyone else. They had to hold a knot on the cord, so that they were out of speaking range of the other prisoners. This harsh idea of punishment was designed as a deterrent.

Document 5: Table of drops, c. 1868

This document is about execution by hanging. It enables the executioner to calculate the length of the drop required to hang a prisoner, based on their weight and height. Prisoners as young as 12 years of age could be hanged for their crimes (depending on the offence committed).

Once you have discussed each document as a class, ask the pupils what they have found surprising or interesting in the documents about different types of punishment. What are the main similarities and differences over time?

Explain that punishments have changed a lot in modern times. Today, in the UK, we no longer have public executions or floggings. The types of crimes being committed have also changed (refer back to the pupils' earlier list from the beginning of the lesson). You could make particular reference to cyber-crime as a relatively 'new' type of criminal activity (with the police and governments also using this technology to hunt down criminals). Today we also have programmes of rehabilitation and reform for prisoners and help for those with mental health problems, and young offenders are not imprisoned with hardened adult criminals but placed in facilities for juvenile offenders.

✏️ Creative activity

Pupils could create posters with illustrations and captions about the different types of punishment over time.

Copyright © Clare Horrie and Rachel Hillman, 2020

☰ Simplified transcript

Henry Munday's prison record

175 Name, No. Henry Munday 5568 17 May 73

4   and aliases

Description

Age (on discharge)	**13**
Height	**4 ft 4 ½**
Hair	**Lt. Brown**
Eyes	**Blue**
Complexion	**Fresh**
Where born	**Clapham**
Married or Single	**Single**
Trade or occupation	**None**
Distinguishing Marks	**None**

Address at time of apprehension **54 Conroy St. Wandsworth Road**

Place and date of conviction **Wandsworth 12 May 73**

Offence for which convicted **Simple Larceny. Stg 14lbs of sugar**

Sentence **4 days H.L. and whipped**

Date to be liberated **15 May 73**

Intended residence after liberation **As above**

Previous Convictions Summary

By Jury

Remarks, antecedents etc

Copyright © Clare Horrie and Rachel Hillman, 2020

📃 Transcript

Table of drops

Executions, table of drops (April 1892)

The length of the drop may usually be calculated by dividing 840 foot-pounds by the weight of the culprit and his clothing in pounds, which will give the length of the drop in feet, but no drop should exceed 8 feet. Thus a person weighing 140 pounds in his clothing will require a drop of 840 divided by 140 = 6 feet. The following table is calculated on this basis up to the weight of 20 pounds:-

Table of drops

Weight of the prisoner in his clothes	Length of the drop		Weight of the prisoner in his clothes	Length of the drop	
lbs	feet	inches	lbs	feet	inches
105 and under	8.	0	142	5.	11
106	7.	11	144	5.	10
107	7.	10	146	5.	9
108	7.	9	148	5.	8
109	7.	8	150	5.	7
110	7.	7	152	5.	6
112	7.	6	155	5.	5
113	7.	5	157	5.	4
114	7.	4	160	5.	3
115	7.	3	162	5.	2
117	7.	2	165	5.	1
118	7.	1	168	5.	0
120	7.	0	170	4.	11
121	6.	11	173	4.	10
123	6.	10	177	4.	9
124	6.	9	180	4.	8
126	6.	8	183	4.	7
127	6.	7	186	4.	6
129	6.	6	189	4.	5
130	6.	5	193	4.	4
132	6.	4	197	4.	3
134	6.	3	201	4.	2
136	6.	2	205	4.	1
138			210	4.	0
140					

When from any special reason, such as diseased condition of neck of the culprit, the Governor and medical officers think that there should be a departure from this table, they may inform the Executioner, and advise him as to the length of the drop which should be given in that particular case.

Copyright © Clare Horrie and Rachel Hillman, 2020

Crime at railway stations

⟳ Lesson overview

Lesson enquiry question

Did the new railways in the 19th century mean more crime?

Resources required

Sources:

❶ Great Northern Railway poster, 1904.

❷ Extract from a report about pickpocketing at King's Cross Station written for the Board of the Great Northern Railway, 1867. All railway companies had a Board of Directors, to which groups or individuals would send reports on the business of the railway.

❸ Extract from a report about the theft of a copper tap at Leeds Station for the Board of the Great Northern Railway.

Other:

• Transcripts for sources 2 and 3.

Lesson focus

Describe:

Describe how the growth of the railway network in Britain was rapid. By the end of Queen Victoria's reign, there were over 1.1 billion passengers using trains.

Explain:

The railway system offered new chances for travel, holidays, transporting goods, and developing businesses and cities. However, railway stations could offer new opportunities for crime.

Curriculum link:

Aspect or theme in British history that extends pupils' chronological knowledge beyond 1066: changes in crime and punishment from the Anglo-Saxons to the present.

❶ Great Northern Railway poster, 1904.

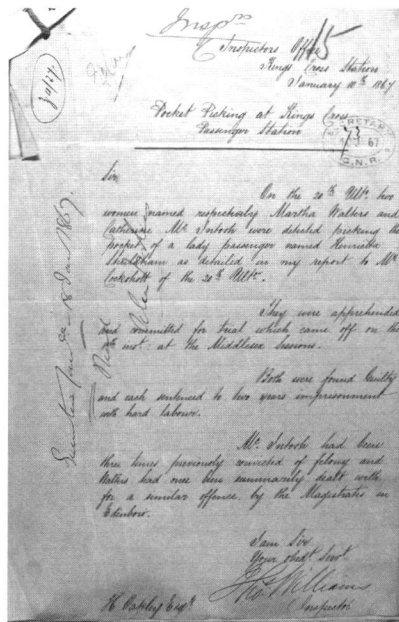

❷ Extract from a report about pickpocketing at King's Cross Station written for the Board of the Great Northern Railway, 1867. All railway companies had a Board of Directors, to which groups or individuals would send reports on the business of the railway.

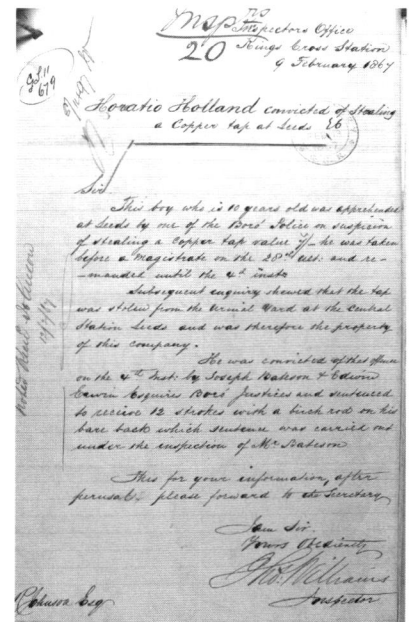

❸ Extract from a report about the theft of a copper tap at Leeds Station for the Board of the Great Northern Railway.

   Copyright © Clare Horrie and Rachel Hillman, 2020

🚀 Starter activity

Give pupils copies of the poster (source 1) or project a large image of it on a whiteboard. Discuss as a class the following:

- What is this source?
- Which railway has made this poster?
- What is the aim of the poster?
- How does this poster persuade people to go on holiday using the train? (Think of the design and how it looks.)
- What special offers does the Northern Railway make?
- How else were people's lives changed by trains, apart from holidays?

⭐ Main activity

Look at source 2 as a mystery document. Pupils work in pairs with a printout or as a class group with a projected image of the document. You can hand out copies of the transcript on page 132 after the pupils have had a go at reading the document. Ask pupils to discuss the following questions:

- What type of document is it?
- Who has written it?
- When was it written?
- What does the heading say this report is about?
- What are the names of the women who carried out the pickpocketing?
- Were they caught?
- What happened when they went to court (Middlesex Sessions)?
- What do you think of their sentence?
- Why do you think these women were punished like this?
- What is the style or tone of the report?
- Why would a railway station offer opportunities for crime? (There are lots of people passing through; there is the distraction of having trains to catch; stations are busy and noisy; people are carrying luggage that is easy to steal; people are carrying money or valuables; a fast getaway would be possible.)

If pupils have been working in pairs, you can now conduct a feedback discussion on their findings.

Now take a look at source 3. This is a very different case of a crime linked to a railway station. See what the pupils can find out from this report. They can either work in pairs with a printout of the source or as a group with the source projected on the whiteboard. Use the following questions as prompts:

- What type of document is it?
- Who has written it?
- When was it written?
- What does the heading say this report is about?
- What was the name of the boy concerned?
- How old was he?
- Does that surprise you?
- Where did he steal the tap from?
- Why do you think he stole it?
- How was he discovered carrying out the crime?
- How was he punished for the crime?
- What do you think of his punishment?
- Why do you think this boy was punished like that?

As a class, discuss whether both of these cases suggest that crime increased because of the railways. Can the pupils think of other reasons why people turned to crime in the 19th century?

✏️ Creative activity

In small groups carry out a mini role play activity based on either or both of these two cases, using roles such as judge, policeman, defendant and witnesses.

📄 Transcript

Extract from a report about pickpocketing at King's Cross Station written for the Board of the Great Northern Railway

Inspectors Office
King's Cross Station

January 10th 1867

Pocket Picking at King's Cross Passenger Station

Sir,

On the 20th ultimo [of last month], two women named respectively Martha Walters and Catherine McIntosh were detected picking the pocket of a lady passenger named Henrietta Shuldham as detailed in my report to Mr Cockshott of the 20th ultimo.

They were apprehended and committed for trial which came off on the 8th instant [present month] at the Middlesex Sessions [law court session].

Both were found guilty and each sentenced to two years imprisonment with hard labour [tiring physical work as punishment].

McIntosh had been three times previously convicted of felony [stealing] and Walters had once been summarily dealt with [come before a court] for a similar offence by the Magistrates in Edinburgh.

I am your obedient servant,

Thomas Williams

Inspector

H. Oakley Esquire

Copyright © Clare Horrie and Rachel Hillman, 2020

Transcript

Extract from a report about the theft of a copper tap at Leeds Station written for the Board of the Great Northern Railway

Inspectors Office
King's Cross Station

9th February 1867

<u>Horatio Holland convicted of stealing a copper tap at Leeds [Station]</u>

Sir,

This boy who is 10 years old was apprehended [stopped] at Leeds by one of the Borough Police on suspicion of stealing a copper tap value 7 shillings. He was taken before a Magistrate [judge] on the 20th ultimo [of last month] and remanded until the 4th instant [kept in custody until the 4th of the present month].

Subsequent enquiry shewed that the tap was stolen from the urinal yard [men's toilets] at the Central Station Leeds and was therefore the property of this Company [Great Northern Railway].

He was convicted of the offence on the 4th instant by Joseph Bateson & Edwin Esquires Borough Justices and sentenced to receive 12 strokes with a birch rod on his bare back which sentence was carried out under the inspection of Mr. Bateson.

This is for your information, after perusal [looking over] please forward [this letter] to the Secretary.

I am Sir,

Yours obediently,

Thomas Williams

Inspector

C. Johnson Esquire

Greek pots 1

⟳ Lesson overview

Lesson enquiry question

What can we learn about the Ancient Greeks from the pots they made?

Resources required

Sources:

❶ A red-figured kylix (drinking cup) showing boys serving wine (front).

❷ View of the kylix from above showing the interior.

Lesson focus

Describe:

Describe how Greek pots give us a window into the lives and beliefs of a people from long ago where there is little or no written record. They reveal figures and scenes from life in Ancient Greece, even animals that the Greeks knew of but might have not seen. Some pots were highly decorated with patterns and others used simple motifs.

Explain:

Explain that Greek pots came in all shapes and sizes to reflect their different uses, from pouring and drinking wine, to carrying and pouring water. They could be used for storing oil, wine or grain. They had different names and were decorated in different ways. Pots are really important in the history of art because they often show detailed images of the human body in movement. There are few large paintings from the time, but pots and sculptures show this development. Greek pottery often shows the human body in realistic ways: fighting, working, eating or resting. The Ancient Greek desire to represent the human form had an important impact on the artists and art that followed them.

Curriculum link:

The legacy of Greek culture (art, architecture or literature) on later periods in British history, including the present day.

❶ A red-figured kylix (drinking cup) showing boys serving wine (front). © The Trustees of the British Museum.

Copyright © Clare Horrie and Rachel Hillman, 2020

🚀 Starter activity

Show the class this short clip to help them find out how the Greeks made their pots: https://smarthistory.org/making-greek-vases.

✏️ Creative activity

Do a Google Image search as a class and make your own display showing as many different designs of Greek pots as you can find, including animals and different types of patterns and scenes. Make a wall chart naming and labelling the different shapes of pots and their uses. These could include storage vessels like amphora, mixing vessels like krater, jugs and cups like kylix, and vases for oils and perfumes, including lekythos.

⭐ Main activity

Look at source 1 as a class and explain to the pupils that this is a Greek kylix or drinking cup. Ask the pupils to look at the scene on the kylix and discuss the following questions:

- What occasion is this?
- How many guests are there?
- Can you describe the hairstyle and clothing of the male at the centre of the pot?
- What are the guests sitting on?
- Can you find some cushions? How are they decorated?
- What are the attendants holding?
- What can you see hanging on the walls? (There are two cups, seen from underneath, and flat-bottomed wine jugs.)
- What pattern can you see near each of the handles of the pot?
- Historians suggest that this pot was used to explain how to hold a symposium, or gathering for noblemen. Can you explain why?

The following information about the scene on the kylix will help you facilitate the discussion. The guests recline on wooden couches propped up with cushions. Jugs and drinking cups are shown hanging up on the wall behind. It shows a symposium, which was important in Ancient Greek culture. A symposium was a private gathering where males met to talk, drink, eat and sing together, and examples of this often appear on pottery decoration.

Now look at source 2, showing the interior of the same kylix. Ask pupils the following questions:

- Can you describe the man pictured on the inside at the bottom of the drinking cup?
- What is he holding?

Now explain that the man was called a komast, a drunken merrymaker. Why do the pupils think this example of Greek pottery contains a joke?

2 View of the kylix from above showing the interior.
© The Trustees of the British Museum.

Greek pots 2

⊙ Lesson overview

Lesson enquiry question

What can we find out from Greek pottery about how they saw their gods?

Resources required

Sources:

❶ A red-figured volute-krater (bowl for mixing wine and water) showing the sacrifice of Iphigeneia (front).

❷ A red-figure bucket pot with black background.

Lesson focus

Describe:

Describe how Greek pots give us a window into the lives and beliefs of a people from long ago where there is little or no written record. They reveal figures and scenes from life in Ancient Greece, even animals that the Greeks knew of but might not have seen. Some pots were highly decorated with patterns and others used simple motifs.

Explain:

Explain that Greek pots came in all shapes and sizes to reflect their different uses, from pouring and drinking wine, to carrying and pouring water. They could be used for storing oil, wine or grain. They had different names and were decorated in different ways. Pots are really important in the history of art because they often show detailed images of the human body in movement. There are few large paintings from the time, but pots and sculptures show this development. Greek pottery often shows the human body in realistic ways: fighting, working, eating or resting. The Ancient Greek desire to represent the human form had an important impact on the artists and art that followed them.

Curriculum link:

The legacy of Greek culture (art, architecture or literature) on later periods in British history, including the present day.

❶ A red-figured volute-krater (bowl for mixing wine and water) showing the sacrifice of Iphigeneia (front). © The Trustees of the British Museum.

❷ A red-figure bucket pot with black background. © The Trustees of the British Museum.

Copyright © Clare Horrie and Rachel Hillman, 2020

🚀 Starter activity

Show the pupils source 1 and discuss the following questions together. Alternatively, the pupils can work in pairs before feeding back to the rest of the group. Tell them this pot is called a volute-krater (a bowl for mixing wine and water).

- Can you describe the patterns used to decorate the pot?
- Why is the pot decorated?
- Can you see:
  - a white altar on two steps
  - Agamemnon, bearded with a sceptre in his left hand and a sacrificial knife in his right hand
  - Iphigeneia (a deer figure) who stands before Agamemnon
  - the goddess Artemis with bow and arrow
  - other figures in the scene?
- Can you explain what is happening?
- What can we learn about the Ancient Greeks from this pot?

Now explain to pupils that the pot probably represents a scene from a play by the Greek Euripides, a tragedy called *Iphigene*. In this scene Agamemnon prepares to sacrifice his daughter Iphigeneia but the goddess Artemis intervenes and turns her into a deer. Artemis was the goddess of wild animals and the hunt, amongst other things. She was also the daughter of Zeus and twin to Apollo, who is shown here seated on the left. In the *Iliad*, Agamemnon was the commander of the Greek forces in the Trojan War. He was the king of Mycenae. There are other versions of this story that the class could research if time permits.

✏️ Creative activity

Ask the pupils to imagine they are a wealthy Greek nobleman wishing to have a pot made for their family, which features the goddess Athena (or another Greek god of their choice). The pupils draw a large outline of their pot, showing the front and back. They write labels for:

- type of pot
- colours
- instructions for the artist for the scenes to be shown
- type of patterns they want, relating to Athena or the goddess or god of their choice.

⭐ Main activity

Now look at source 2 and ask the pupils to discuss the following questions:

- Can you draw a simple outline of the shape of this pot?
- How is it decorated?
- This type of pot is a situla, a bucket. Do the handles tell us anything about what it was used for?
- What clothes and jewellery is the figure on the left wearing?
- Do you know who it is? (She's Athena.)
- What is behind her?
- Can you describe the clothes worn by the figure on the right?
- What weapons does he have?
- Do these suggest who he is? (He's Perseus.)
- How is he positioned?
- What is he being given by Athena? (A harpe or curved sword.)
- What do you think this scene means?
- Why do you think the Greeks showed stories about their gods on their pots?

Explain to pupils that the pot shows the hero Perseus receiving the harpe (a special type of sword resembling a sickle, used to kill Medusa) from the goddess Athena. He is seated on a rock facing her. There are simple star and palm shapes above the two figures.

The myth of Perseus and Medusa has provided powerful inspiration for many artists and sculptors in ancient times and beyond. Medusa was one of three sisters, the Gorgons, whom Poseidon had turned into monsters with live snakes covering their heads. Medusa kept her beautiful face and whoever looked at it was turned to stone. Perseus had been set the impossible task by King Polydectes to bring back her head. He asked Athena and Hermes for help. They gave him winged sandals to fly to the Gorgons' home, a cap that made him invisible, a sword (harpe), which is shown on the pot, and a mirrored shield. The shield meant he could see a reflection of Medusa's face and avoid being turned into stone. Perseus was then able to cut off her head by looking at the reflection in the shield. He managed to escape and later used Medusa's head as a weapon in battle.

The pupils can now research further the lives of Athena and Perseus individually or in pairs.

Early railways

⊙ Lesson overview

Lesson enquiry question

How much did it cost to build one of the earliest railways?

Resources required

Sources:

❶ Drawing of George Stephenson's Rocket engine produced in 1894.

❷ Document to show the cost of the Liverpool to Manchester Railway as estimated by George Stephenson, 5th February 1825.

Other:

- Transcript for source 2.
- Map of Britain, to show the location of Liverpool and Manchester.

Lesson focus

Describe:

Describe how George Stephenson (1781–1848) built the 'Rocket' railway engine in 1829 for use on one of the first passenger railways in Britain.

Explain:

Explain that George Stephenson was a self-educated engineer who designed the Liverpool to Manchester Railway, which opened in 1830 although building had started in the 1820s. It was the first railway to completely run on steam power and have a signalling system.

Curriculum link:

A significant turning point in British history: the first railways.

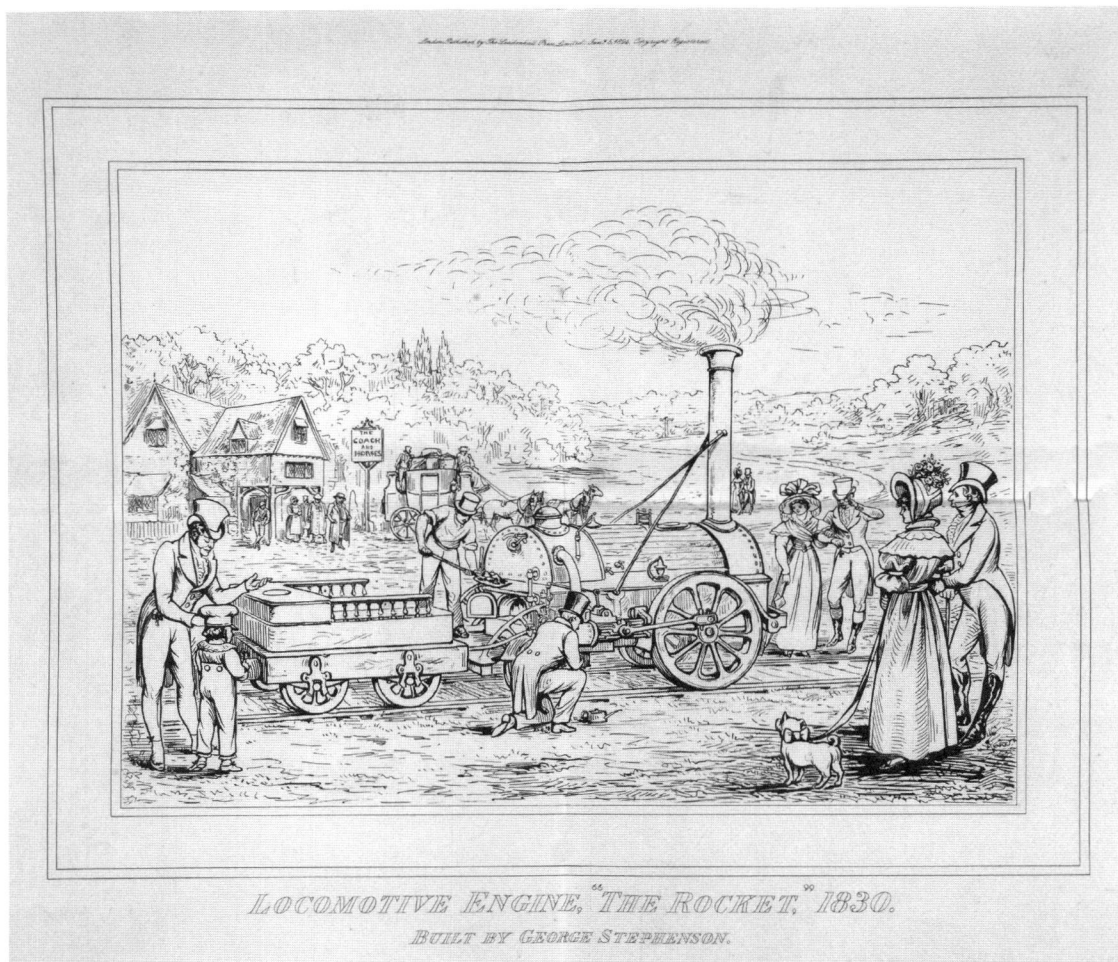

❶ Drawing of George Stephenson's Rocket engine produced in 1894.

   Copyright © Clare Horrie and Rachel Hillman, 2020

2 Document to show the cost of the Liverpool to Manchester Railway as estimated by George Stephenson, 5th February 1825.

🚀 Starter activity

Show the pupils the drawing of the 'Rocket' (source 1). Discuss the following:

- What two types of transport can you see?
- Why do you think people might want to travel by railway?
- What do you think it might have been like to travel on an early railway?
- Why do you think Stephenson's engine was called the 'Rocket'?

⭐ Main activity

Now look at source 2 as a class and discuss these questions:

- What type of document is it?
- Who has written it?
- What are the two biggest costs?
- Why was money needed for fences and bridges?
- Why was an Act of Parliament needed to build the line? What did it cost?
- How many engines were needed to run on the railway?
- What is the total cost of the railway?
- Why does it cost so much?
- Use this currency converter to work out what it would cost today: www.nationalarchives.gov.uk/currency-converter.

✏️ Creative activity

Using the information in source 2, pupils draw a plan of the railway, adding labels, diagrams and pictures that explain the cost to build it.

📄 Transcript

Document to show the cost of the Liverpool to Manchester Railway

This is a document to show the cost of the Liverpool to Manchester Railway, as estimated by its engineer and designer, George Stephenson. The railway was opened in 1830, but building had started in the 1820s. It was the first railway to completely run on steam power and have a signalling system. The document is dated 5th February 1825.

Estimate of the Expense of the proposed Rail Road from the Port of Liverpool to the Town of Manchester

Forming Excavation & embankments	37,599	2	5
Bridges & other masonry	16,920		
Stone Blocks at ¼ each	15,957	6	8
Chairs or pedestals 10lbs each at 15 £ per ton	16,028	12	6
Rail, 4 lines of 35lbs per yard for 34 miles at £16.10 per ton	61,710		
Laying Rails & forming Road for 34 miles at 5/- per yard	14,960		
Fencing the Road	5,129	8	
Gates 400 @ £1.10 shillings each	600		
Waggons for making the Road	4,000		
Locomotive Engine 20 @ 600 £ each	12,000		
Boilers on the Road	1,500		
Cranes & machinery at the wharfs	2,000		
Warehouses & Offices	25,000		
Land	100,000		
Surveys & Act of Parliament	10,000		
Contingencies during the performance of the work	26,595	10	5
	£400,000		

George Stephenson
February 5th 1825

Copyright © Clare Horrie and Rachel Hillman, 2020

Blackout Britain: Hiding the coastline

⟳ Lesson overview

Lesson enquiry question

Why did Britain try to hide the coastline during the Second World War?

Resources required

Sources:

❶ Extracts from a memorandum by the First Lord of the Admiralty to the War Cabinet, October 1941.

❷ A public information poster warning about road accidents in the dark.

Other:

• Transcript for Source 1.

Lesson focus

Describe:

Describe the measures taken by the British government in the Second World War to hide the coastline so it couldn't be seen from the air.

Explain:

Explain why Britain needed to take these measures to hide its coastline.

Curriculum link:

A significant turning point in British history.

Coal Dust Films for Camouflage of Coastlines.

Memorandum by the First Lord of the Admiralty.

In Battle of the Atlantic, S/50/79, Second Meeting, Conclusion 1, the Admiralty, in conjunction with the Ministry of Home Security, were directed to experiment with the camouflage of tidal water by the application of coal dust.

2. The Appendix attached summarizes the results of the trials which have been carried out.

3. If the process is to be applied on the large scale required for the camouflage of major waterways or commercial port areas, the number of craft and personnel would be very large, and the quantity of coal which would have to be transported would be prohibitive. For example, to cover the Mersey alone, and outside the docks, would require a monthly consumption of 200,000 tons of coal, and the employment of at least 400 mobile units. This consumption is based on 10 moonlight nights of 10 hours each.

4. The coal will have to go somewhere once it has been placed on the water. Some will be carried away by the tide, some will sink, and a little may remain temporarily suspended. The quantities involved will represent considerable siltage in rivers and estuaries which have already to be continually dredged to keep them clear. The

6. In view of the large numbers of craft and personnel, and the great quantities of material, required, it seems doubtful whether this method will be a practical proposition.

❶ Extracts from a memorandum by the First Lord of the Admiralty to the War Cabinet, October 1941.

2 A public information poster warning about road accidents in the dark.

🚀 Starter activity

Treat source 1 as a mystery document, telling the pupils only that it is a document that describes a special wartime experiment to help protect Britain from attack. Show the pupils the source and ask them the following questions:

· What was the main idea behind this experiment?
· Why did it not work?
· Why would it have been a waste of coal in wartime?
· What do think it showed about the government?
· Why might people today object to such plans?

The following information about the source will help you to guide the discussion. The source describes an experiment that would make enemy bombing difficult with Hitler's plan to invade Britain in the Second World War. It is a note from the head of the Navy to the War Cabinet describing an experiment to use coal dust to disguise the outline of the coastline and other inland waterways and rivers, making it difficult for German bombers to attack ports, docks and estuaries. The film of coal dust would cut out any reflection from the water and make it less visible.

⭐ Main activity

Explain that the government also made everyone in the country black out all signs of light at night to prevent towns, cities and factories being seen from the air at night and therefore targeted by German bombers.

Pupils work in pairs to examine the poster and answer the following questions:

· Can you explain why the poster has a cat on it?
· What is the message of the poster?
· Does it get the message over clearly?
· What do you think about the design?
· What would you expect most people to complain about when preparing for the blackout?

To conclude the activity, conduct a feedback discussion with the whole class on their findings.

✏️ Creative activity

The class make a set of illustrated postcards to explain any proverbs that they know or can research, for example: 'A stitch in time saves nine'; 'Don't judge a book by its cover'; 'Don't cry over spilt milk.'

Copyright © Clare Horrie and Rachel Hillman, 2020

📄 Transcript

Extracts from a memorandum by the First Lord of the Admiralty to the War Cabinet, October 1941

Coal Dust Films for Camouflage of Coastlines

Memorandum by the First Lord of the Admiralty.

In Battle of the Atlantic, S/50/79, Second Meeting, Conclusion 1, the Admiralty, in conjunction [together] with the Ministry of Home Security, were directed to experiment with the camouflage of tidal water by the application [using] of coal dust.

2. The appendix attached summarizes the results which have been carried out.

3. If the process is to be applied on the large scale required for the camouflage of major waterways or commercial port areas, the number of craft [boats] and personnel would be very large, and the quantity of coal which would have to be transported would be prohibitive [not worth it]. For example to cover the Mersey alone, and outside the docks, would require a monthly consumption of 200,000 tons of coal, and the employment of at least 400 mobile units. This consumption is based on 10 moonlight nights of 10 hours each.

…

4. The coal will have to go somewhere once it is has been placed on the water. Some will be carried away by the tide, some will sink, and a little may remain temporarily suspended. The quantities involved will represent considerable siltage in rivers and estuaries which have already to be continually dredged to keep them clear.

…

6. In view of the large numbers of craft and personnel, and the great quantities of material required, it seems doubtful whether this method will be a practical proposition.

Lesson 46

Blackout Britain: The problems caused

⊙ Lesson overview

Lesson enquiry question

Blackout Britain: What problems were caused by the blackout?

Resources required

Sources:

1 Extract from notes for a debate in the House of Commons about blackouts on 23rd January 1940.

2 A road safety poster: 'Lookout in the blackout' by Pat Keely, c. 1940.

Other:

- Transcript for Source 1.

Lesson focus

Describe:

Describe the problems caused by the blackout, including traffic accidents, difficulties involving public transport and increasing numbers of burglaries.

Explain:

Explain what the government did to remind the British people about safety during the blackout.

Curriculum link:

A significant turning point in British history.

> 2. By far the greater part of the fatal accidents take place during the "black-out". Figures were obtained specially for October, November and December to show the number of persons killed during the "hours of darkness" (i.e. the "black-out") and are as follows:-
>
> | | Hours of Darkness. | "Other" hours. | Total. |
> |---|---|---|---|
> | October | 564 | 355 | 919 |
> | November | 674 | 252 | 926 |
> | December | 896 | 260 | 1,156 |
>
> The "black-out" casualties increase as the days grow shorter.

1 Extract from notes for a debate in the House of Commons about blackouts on 23rd January 1940.

Copyright © Clare Horrie and Rachel Hillman, 2020

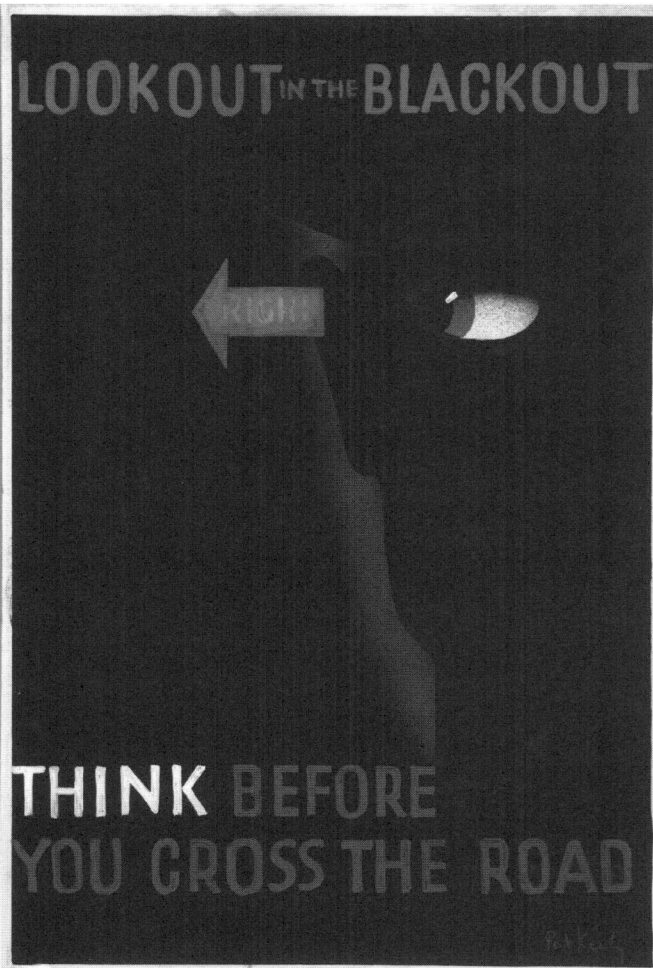

2 A road safety poster: 'Lookout in the blackout' by Pat Keely, c. 1940.

Starter activity

Read through source 1 together on a whiteboard or by handing out printed copies to the pupils. You can use the transcript if needed but only after pupils have had a go at reading the original text. Discuss with the pupils:

- How many people died from road accidents during the 'hours of darkness' in the whole of October 1939?
- What is being blamed for the rise in accidents?
- Can you explain why?

Main activity

You can now explain to the pupils that this source shows concerns about accidents caused as a result of the blackout because of the lack of street lighting and the dimmed traffic lights. During the Second World War the government wanted to make it difficult for German bombers to attack cities, ports and docks. Therefore, everyone in the country blacked out all signs of light at night to stop towns and cities and factories being seen from the air. To help prevent accidents during the blackout, white stripes were painted on the roads and on lampposts. Volunteers were trained as air raid precaution (ARP) wardens, checking that householders had put out the light. Windows had to have blackout curtains. Pedestrians were asked to carry newspapers or a white handkerchief to make them more visible. The elderly were advised to keep off the streets after dark. Rail travel, too, was complicated by the blackout. In railway yards, porters found it hard to read labels on goods travelling by train at night, which resulted in delays for passengers. Rail passengers had to sit in darkened carriages patrolled by lighting attendants with torches. Bus numbers were unlit, which also made travel difficult. Burglary also increased because of the blackout. The blackout was used in other countries during the war too. In Britain it ended in April 1945.

Pupils can now work in pairs to examine the poster (source 2). Ask them to think about the following questions:

- Can you describe the poster?
- What is the message of the poster?
- Can you explain why or why not the message is clear?
- How effective is the design? Think about the use of colour and text too.

You can now conduct a feedback discussion on the pupils' findings. Explain that the 'lookout in the blackout' campaign first originated in February 1940, due to the number of fatal accidents in the blackout. The campaign used posters to remind people about safety.

Creative activity

Imagine you are living in Britain during the Second World War. Write a letter to the government describing the problems you face during the blackout.

Copyright © Clare Horrie and Rachel Hillman, 2020

Transcript

Extract from a debate in the House of Commons about blackouts in January 1940

2. By far the greater part of the fatal accidents [when people die] take place during the "black-out". Figures were obtained specially for October, November and December to show the number of persons killed during the "hours of darkness" (i.e. the "black-out") and are as follows:-

	Hours of Darkness	"Other" hours	Total
October	564	355	919
November	674	252	926
December	896	260	1,156

The "black-out" casualties increase as the days grow shorter.

[Note: this is in the winter months when the clocks 'go back an hour' so that it gets darker earlier in the evening and lighter in the morning.]

Copyright © Clare Horrie and Rachel Hillman, 2020

Blackout Britain: Road safety posters

⟳ Lesson overview

Lesson enquiry question

Blackout Britain: What can we learn from road safety posters in the Second World War?

Resources required

Sources:

❶ A road safety poster by Tom Gentleman, 1943.

❷ A road safety poster by Pat Keely, possibly 1941.

Lesson focus

Describe:

Describe how posters were used as part of a government campaign to improve safety during the blackout due to concerns about increased accidents caused as a result of its introduction.

Explain:

Explain how road safety posters can tell us about day-to-day life during the blackout and the adjustments people had to make.

Curriculum link:

A significant turning point in British history.

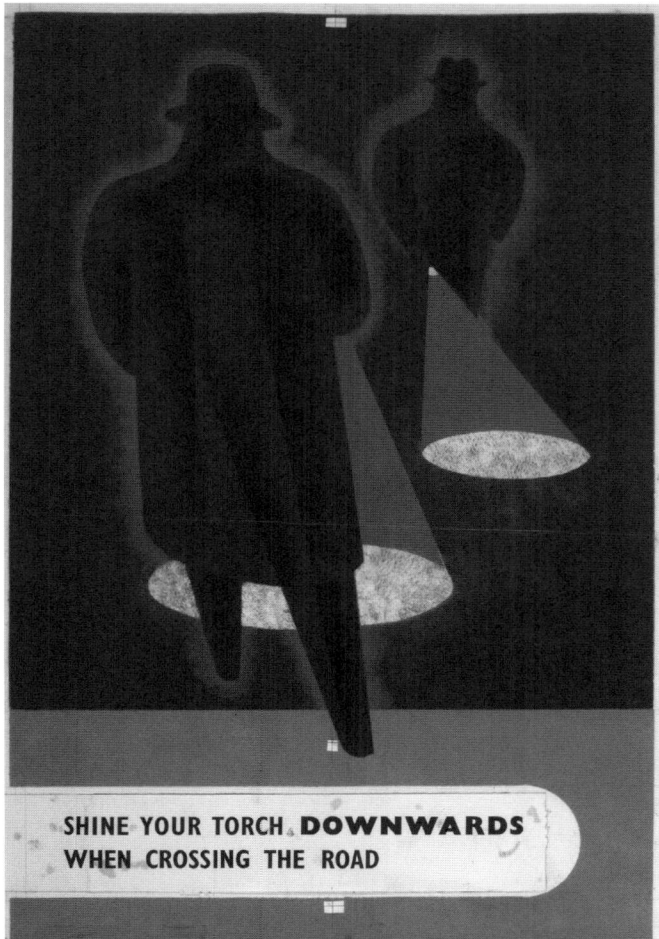

SHINE YOUR TORCH DOWNWARDS WHEN CROSSING THE ROAD

❶ A road safety poster by Tom Gentleman, 1943.

Copyright © Clare Horrie and Rachel Hillman, 2020

🚀 Starter activity

Project source 1 on a whiteboard or print and hand out copies to the pupils. Discuss the following:

- What can you see in the poster?
- What is the message of the poster?
- How would this advice make roads safer?
- Does it get the message over clearly?
- What do you think about the design?
- Would you change it at all?

You can explain to the pupils that this is a poster in a strong modern graphic style, depicting two shadowy civilian men shining their torch as they cross each other in the road. The slogan is direct: 'Shine your torch downwards when crossing the road'. This would avoid blinding drivers and other pedestrians in the blacked-out streets.

⭐ Main activity

Pupils now work in pairs to examine the second poster (source 2). Give them the following questions to support their observations:

- What can you see in the poster?
- What is the message of the poster?
- What do you think about the use of colour in the poster?
- Does it get the message over clearly?
- What do you think about the design?

You can then bring the pupils back together for a feedback discussion on their findings. Explain that the poster shows a civilian man wearing a white armband crossing at a green wartime street crossing light. The text colours, amber and green, suggest the colour of traffic lights, giving the signal for a go-ahead when appropriate. The government encouraged people to wear the white armband shown in this poster but found out that only seven per cent of people wore it or carried something white.

✏️ Creative activity

As a class, think about what other adjustments people may have had to make to their everyday lives to ensure safety during the blackout. Pupils can design their own blackout poster to advertise one of these adjustments.

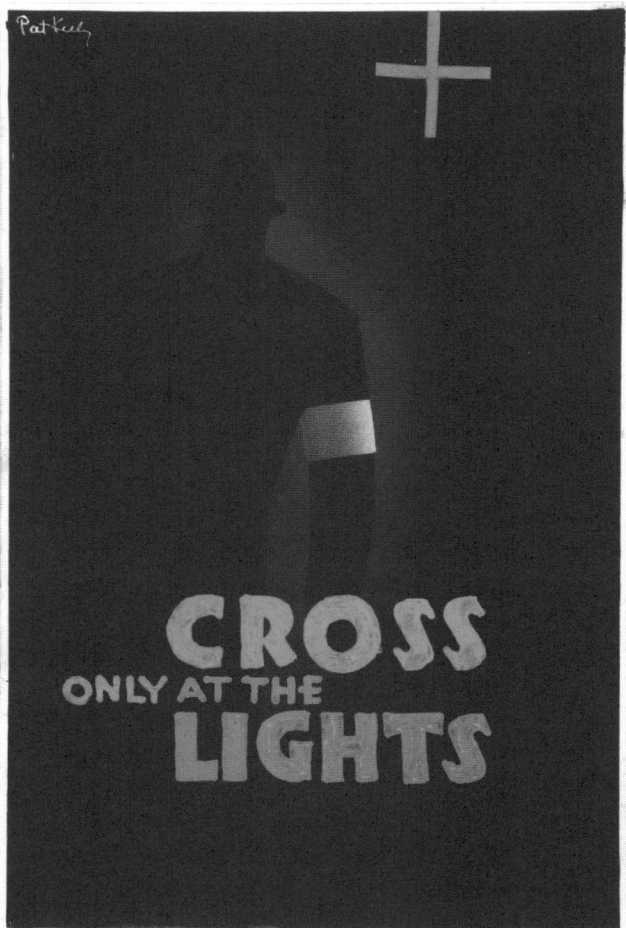

❷ A road safety poster by Pat Keely, possibly 1941.

Copyright © Clare Horrie and Rachel Hillman, 2020

Britain Blitzed 1

⟳ Lesson overview

Lesson enquiry question

How can we find out about the Blitz?

Resources required

Sources:

❶ Poster created by the National Savings Committee campaign during the Second World War to encourage people to buy war bonds, 1940.

❷ Photograph called 'Canteen work in a bombed area', publicity material, 1941–1942.

Lesson focus

Describe:

Describe what two sources can help us find out about the Blitz.

Explain:

Explain that the Blitz (1940–1941) was a German bombing campaign against Britain during the Second World War. The British press first used the term 'Blitz', the German word for 'lightning'.

Curriculum link:

A significant turning point in British history.

❶ Poster created by the National Savings Committee campaign during the Second World War to encourage people to buy war bonds, 1940.

🚀 Starter activity

Project the poster (source 1) onto a whiteboard. Ask the class to jot down anything they notice about the picture. You can use the following questions as prompts if needed:

- Who are the people in the picture?
- Can you explain their jobs?
- What damage can you see?

Explain that the poster was used as part of a government saving scheme. Ask the pupils if they can think why the government might want to encourage people to save with them. (The government would be able to use the money invested in the form of savings to rebuild the country after the damage done due to the war.) Once pupils are clear on this, ask them how this helps us understand about the Blitz.

⭐ Main activity

Now ask the class to examine in pairs the photograph (source 2) and discuss what they can see. Offer the following questions if they need some prompts to support their observations:

- Who are the people in the picture?
- What are they doing?
- What damage can you see?

Bring the pupils back together and ask them to feed back on their findings. Now ask the pupils to think back to the first poster they saw in the starter activity and draw comparisons between the two posters:

- What is the difference between the two sources?
- Which is more useful to a historian?
- How could you find out more about the Blitz?
- What other sources could you use?

✏️ Creative activity

Have a look at some Blitz safety posters online together as a class. The pupils can now make their own poster advising people how to stay safe in the Blitz.

❷ Photograph called 'Canteen work in a bombed area', publicity material, 1941–1942.

Copyright © Clare Horrie and Rachel Hillman, 2020

Britain Blitzed 2

⟳ Lesson overview

Lesson enquiry question

How can we find out about the Blitz?

Resources required

Source:

❶ Photograph of bomb damage.

Lesson focus

Describe:

Describe how a photographic source can help us find out about the Blitz.

Explain:

Explain that the Blitz (1940–1941) was a German bombing campaign against Britain during the Second World War. The British press first used the term 'Blitz', the German word for 'lightning'.

Curriculum link:

A significant turning point in British history.

🚀 Starter activity

Project the photograph onto a whiteboard. Ask the pupils to jot down anything they notice. The photograph shows bombed housing and damage, but the shelters seem to be still standing at D, F and G.

Pupils should make a list of as many descriptive words as they can to describe the photograph. Now discuss:

- What does the photograph reveal?
- Why do you think this picture was taken?
- Who could have taken it?

⭐ Main activity

Split the class into pairs. Ask the pupils to think about the following questions:

- How could you use this photograph to persuade people to use shelters?
- Why do you think some houses were hit and some survived?
- What can this tell you about the nature of bombing raids?
- Why are photographs useful to historians?
- How could you find out more about the Blitz?

Conclude the activity with a whole-class discussion.

❶ Photograph of bomb damage.

✏ Creative activity

The pupils use the list of descriptive words they came up with in the starter activity in a poem or short piece of writing about the bomb damage shown in the photograph.

Britain Blitzed 3

⊙ Lesson overview

Lesson enquiry question

How can we find out about the Blitz?

Resources required

Sources:

❶ Extract from a Home Office government report on Morrison shelters.

❷ Diagram of Morrison shelter.

Other:

• Transcript and simplified transcript for source 1.

Lesson focus

Describe:

Describe the indoor Morrison shelter, common during the Blitz, using a report and a diagram.

Explain:

Explain that there were different types of shelter used during the Blitz, including Anderson shelters in people's gardens, Morrison shelters used inside, and public shelters in basements, railway arches and London Tube stations.

Curriculum link:

A significant turning point in British history.

During the recent raid on York Mr. McGregor aged 79, his wife of 78 and an airman on leave owe their lives to the fact that they were in a "Morrison" when their house collapsed as a result of a direct hit. They were stunned, but soon came out of the shelter, without help. Mrs. McGregor had a slight hand injury and the airman cuts on the head and shoulder; Mr. McGregor received no injury. The shelter which had saved their lives was tilted but it held off the debris of the two storey building. (See photo 4).

A report of Ministry of Home Security experts on 39 cases of bombing incidents in different parts of Britain covering all those for which full particulars are available in which Morrison shelters were involved shows how well they have stood up to severe tests of heavy bombing.

All the incidents were serious. Many of the incidents involved direct hits on the houses concerned a risk against which it was never claimed these shelters would afford protection. In all of them the houses in which shelters were placed were within the radius of damage by bombs; in 24 there was complete demolition of the house on the shelter.

A hundred and nineteen people were sheltering in these "Morrisons" and only four were killed. So that 115 out of 119 people were saved. Of these only 7 were seriously injured and 14 slightly injured while 94 escaped uninjured. The majority were able to leave their shelters unaided.

❶ Extract from a Home Office government report on Morrison shelters.

 Copyright © Clare Horrie and Rachel Hillman, 2020

🚀 Starter activity

Read through the government document about Morrison shelters as a class. Once the pupils have had a go at reading the original text, you can offer them copies of the transcript if required. There is also a simplified version that can be offered, depending on the abilities in your group. Discuss the following questions with the pupils:

- Did Morrison shelters save lives during Second World War air raids by German aircraft?
- How well did the Morrison shelter stand up to heavy bombing?
- Could it save people in a direct hit upon a house?
- Why would the government write a report on shelters?

⭐ Main activity

In pairs, the pupils examine source 2. You can explain to them that it is a diagram of a Morrison shelter. Ask them to discuss the following questions:

- Do you think it was difficult to put a Morrison shelter together?
- As well as being an indoor air raid shelter, how else could the Morrison shelter be used?
- Why is this diagram useful to people finding out about the Blitz?
- What other sources could you use to find out more?

Conduct a feedback discussion on the pupils' findings to conclude the activity.

✏️ Creative activity

Find pictures of other types of air raid shelter and show them to the pupils. The pupils can then write a diary entry describing a night in any one of these types of shelter during an air raid. They should describe the whole event, including getting to the shelter, any explosions that took place, what it was like inside the shelter, what happened at the end of the raid and any damage that was caused during the raid. They should write about how they felt during the air raid.

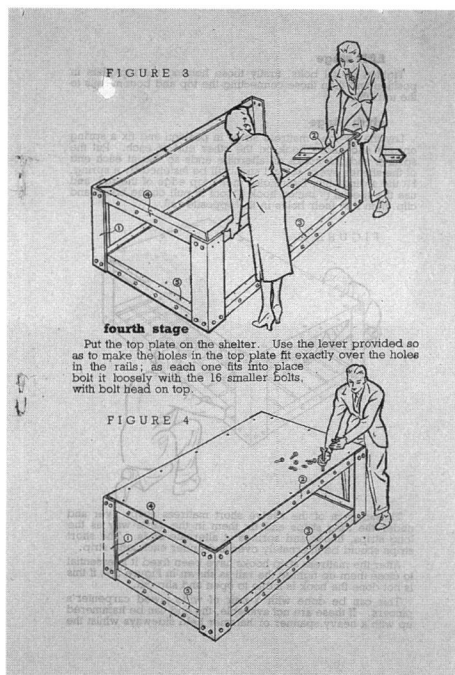

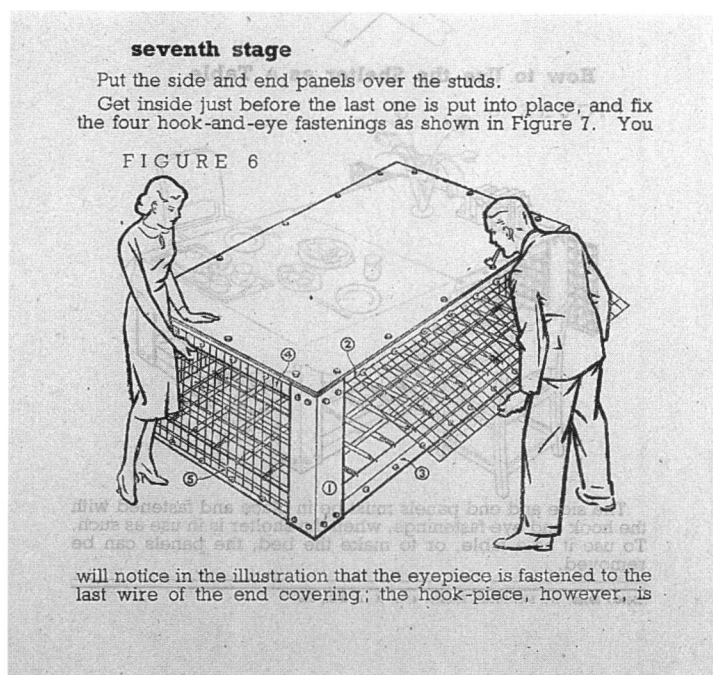

2 Diagram of Morrison shelter.

📄 Transcript

Extract from a Home Office government report on the effectiveness of Morrison shelters

During the recent raid on York Mr. McGregor aged 79, his wife of 78 and an airman on leave owe their lives to the fact that they were in a "Morrison" when their house collapsed as a result of a direct hit. They were stunned, but soon came out of the shelter, without help. Mrs. McGregor had a slight hand injury and the airman cuts on the head and shoulder; Mr. McGregor received no injury. The shelter which had saved their lives was tilted but it held off the debris of the two storey building.

A report of Ministry of Home Security experts on 39 cases of bombing incidents in different parts of Britain covering all those for which full particulars are available in which Morrison shelters were involved shows how well they have stood up to severe tests of heavy bombing.

All the incidents were serious. Many of the incidents involved direct hits on the houses concerned a risk against which it was never claimed these shelters would afford protection. In all of them the houses in which shelters were placed were within the radius of damage by bombs; in 24 there was complete demolition of the house on the shelter.

A hundred and nineteen people were sheltering in these "Morrisons" and only four were killed. So that 115 out of 119 people were saved. Of these only 7 were seriously injured and 14 slightly injured while 94 escaped uninjured. The majority were able to leave their shelters unaided.

Copyright © Clare Horrie and Rachel Hillman, 2020

Simplified transcript

Extract from a Home Office government report on the effectiveness of Morrison shelters

In a raid in York, Mr and Mrs McGregor owe their lives to the Morrison shelter when their house collapsed on them in a direct hit. They were not badly hurt apart from some minor injuries.

The government says in 39 cases the Morrison shelter has stood up to heavy bombing raids and in 24 of these cases the house was completely destroyed.

Out of 119 people, only 4 in Morrison shelters were killed. Most were able to walk out of their shelters without help after a raid.

Tutankhamun

⟳ Lesson overview

Lesson enquiry question

What can documents tell us about the discovery of Tutankhamun?

Resources required

Sources:

1. Photograph relating to the discovery of Tutankhamun's tomb.
2. Plan of Valley of the Kings.
3. Antechamber of Tutankhamun's tomb.
4. Sarcophagus of Tutankhamun.

Other:

- Bag of props relating to the discovery of Tutankhamun's tomb.

Lesson focus

Describe:

Describe who Tutankhamun was.

Explain:

Explain what was discovered inside Tutankhamun's tomb and what these items can reveal about the Pharaoh.

Curriculum link:

Events beyond living memory: finding out about the discovery of Tutankhamun's tomb.

1 Photograph relating to the discovery of Tutankhamun's tomb.

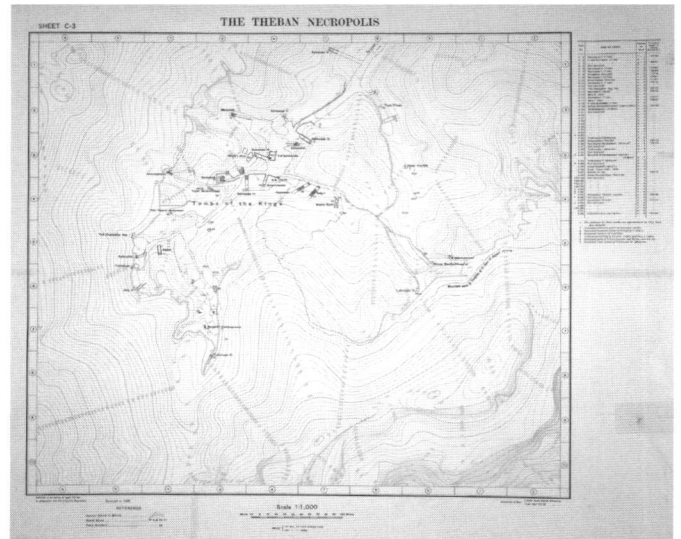

2 Plan of Valley of the Kings.

Copyright © Clare Horrie and Rachel Hillman, 2020

🚀 Starter activity

Display the image of Valley of the Kings (source 1) on the whiteboard or give pupils copies to look at. Ask the pupils to take a few minutes just to look at the document and then feed back on the things that they can see. Possible questions that you could ask are:

- What type of document is this?
- What can you see in the document? (They should be able to pick out mountains, people, sand, rubble and a tomb.)
- What do you think this is a photo of? (They should be able to work out that it might be a burial place and some pupils might even recognise it as Valley of the Kings.)

Explain to the pupils that this is a holiday photograph taken by a man called Ramsay MacDonald (Labour prime minister) on his holiday during the mid 1920s. The photograph shows the tombs of Ramesses II and Ramesses III, pharaohs of Ancient Egypt. Explain that at this time there was a lot of interest in Ancient Egypt and the study of Egypt (Egyptology). Archaeological excavations were taking place in Egypt and all over the world, which had led to some very exciting discoveries. This included one of the most famous discoveries of all time. Do the pupils know what this might be?

Find out what the pupils know already about Tutankhamun and Ancient Egypt. Then tell them the story of Tutankhamun and draw on some of the key points below:

- In Ancient Egypt, in the New Kingdom (1504–1069 BC), pharaohs were buried in the Valley of the Kings, which has lots of tunnels deep underground.
- Tutankhamun reigned over 3,000 years ago in Egypt.
- He was the son of King Akhenaten.
- Tutankhamun became pharaoh at nine years old and he married his half-sister Ankhesenamun.
- Tutankhamun was about 18 or 19 years old when he died and no one knows for certain the cause of his death. Some say that he was murdered and others argue that he died of natural causes. It is agreed that because he died suddenly and unexpectedly his tomb was prepared in a hurry.

Explain that Ancient Egyptians believed that life continued in the afterlife, so they mummified their dead and they furnished the tomb with all that was needed. You can explain mummification to the pupils using the following notes.

- All Ancient Egyptians, including pharaohs, were mummified when they died.
- The procedure was carried out by a priest who wore the jackal-headed mask of Anubis (god of the dead).
- The person's body was washed and prepared. The lungs and intestines were removed, washed, packed in salt and placed in special canopic jars. The brain was removed through the nose using a long hook.

❸ Antechamber of Tutankhamun's tomb. © Hulton Archive/Getty Images.

❹ Sarcophagus of Tutankhamun. © DEA / G. DAGLI ORTI/ De Agostini via Getty Images.

Copyright © Clare Horrie and Rachel Hillman, 2020

- The body, covered in salt, was then left for 40 days.
- The body was stuffed with material then wrapped in linen before the funeral.
- Religious rituals performed at the funeral included the 'opening of the mouth' ceremony so the deceased could speak, hear, see and eat in the afterlife.

⭐ Main activity

Tell the pupils that one of the biggest mysteries that puzzled historians and archaeologists for many years was 'Where was Tutankhamun's tomb?' Explore the story of the discovery of the tomb as described below, using the pupils to help act out events and a story bag of props to illustrate your retelling. Props could include a trowel and a large paintbrush for excavating, a smart hat for Lord Carnarvon, a battery-operated candle to explore the tomb, and replica treasure for the contents of the tomb.

In 1907, Lord Carnarvon, a wealthy Englishman, hired Howard Carter to lead the excavation of an Ancient Egyptian tomb, where they thought Tutankhamun had been buried. In 1914 Carnarvon secured the right to dig, but then the outbreak of the First World War interrupted their work and they had to stop excavating.

They started digging again in 1917, but by 1922 they still hadn't found anything. Carnarvon was quite frustrated by this and said he would only fund the dig for one final year.

On 4th November 1922, Carter and his team slowly uncover a flight of stone steps that takes them to a tomb sealed by a heavy, stone door. Carter makes a small hole in the door, and peers inside. He exclaims to everyone that he can see 'wonderful things' inside!

The team have found the tomb of Tutankhamun and spend many months cataloguing their findings. Carter becomes quite a celebrity and tours America lecturing about his findings.

Explain that in this lesson, pupils are going to become archaeologists like Howard Carter. They are going to enter the tomb of Tutankhamun and carefully examine documents and photographs about the discovery to find out what was concealed inside. Pinpoint Tutankhamun's tomb on Source 2, a plan of Valley of the Kings, as surveyed in 1926, to help bring this to life. Give the pupils the following images and ask them to answer the questions in pairs. Once the pupils have examined both photographs, gather them together and ask them to feed back their findings. You can use the description of each image to guide the discussion.

The antechamber

Questions:

- Describe what you can see in the photograph.
- List some of the objects that you can spot. What might these have been used for? Why have they been placed inside Tutankhamun's tomb?
- What does this photograph tell us about the importance of Tutankhamun?

Description:

The antechamber was the gateway to all of the other rooms in Tutankhamun's tomb. Although the contents of the antechamber look grand, it was considered quite a modest space and room of belongings for a pharaoh. This is said to have been because Tutankhamun had such a short life and an untimely death, so there wasn't time to prepare this space properly.

The sarcophagus

Questions:

- Describe what you can see in the photograph.
- What do you think this object was used for? What is it made out of?
- What does this object reveal about Tutankhamun and how he was viewed by his people?

Description:

Tutankhamun had three coffins made of wood, all housed inside each other for protection. The final coffin that contained Tutankhamun's mummy was made of solid gold.

Explain how Carter and his team had to carefully photograph and sketch each discovery they made to document their findings. Their discovery was the first time that a royal Egyptian mummy had been found completely undisturbed since it had been buried over 3,000 years ago!

🖊 Creative activity

Explain to the pupils that Egyptian kings were buried with special possessions that they would use in the afterlife, such as toys, figures or servants. Pupils could draw the special possessions that they would have put into Tutankhamun's tomb, based on what they've found out about him during the lesson and any other research they would like to do about his life.

Copyright © Clare Horrie and Rachel Hillman, 2020

Ancient Egyptian beliefs

⟳ Lesson overview

Lesson enquiry question

What do the artefacts reveal about Ancient Egyptian beliefs in the afterlife?

Resources required

Sources:

1 Funeral procession, Ani's Book of the Dead.

2 Weighing of the heart of Ani.

3 Equipment for the opening of the mouth ceremony.

Other:

- Worksheet: Layers of inference. Photocopy one per pair.
- Mini whiteboards.

Lesson focus

Describe:

Describe some of the different images used in Ani's Book of the Dead and the meaning behind them.

Explain:

Explain some of the different rituals that were performed to enter the afterlife.

Curriculum link:

An overview of where and when the first civilisations appeared and conduct a depth study of one of the following: Ancient Sumer, The Indus Valley, Ancient Egypt, The Shang Dynasty of Ancient China.

1 Funeral procession, Ani's Book of the Dead. © The Trustees of the British Museum.

2 Weighing of the heart of Ani. © CM Dixon/Print Collector/Getty Images.

3 Equipment for the opening of the mouth ceremony. © The Trustees of the British Museum.

🚀 Starter activity

Display the image of the funeral procession (source 1) on the whiteboard. Ask the pupils to take a few minutes looking at the image in pairs and writing down what they can see on mini whiteboards. Encourage the pupils to talk about what the people are wearing and what they might be holding. Also get them to look carefully at the top half and then the bottom half of the document. How are they different? Why are they different? (The bottom half is made up of Egyptian hieroglyphics.) Some of the pairs can then share their ideas with the class.

Now ask the pupils to discuss the following questions in their pairs, again writing down their responses:

- When do you think the document was made? Why?
- Where do you think the document was made? Why?
- What do you think the people in the image are doing?

Encourage the pupils to link their inferences in response to these questions back to their initial observations. Once the pupils have had an opportunity to feed back their observations and inferences, explain to them that they are looking at an image of an Ancient Egyptian funeral procession. It's taken from 'The Book of the Dead', a dead person's guide to the afterlife and the dangers they would face on the way. A collection of spells written in hieroglyphs, it was placed in or near the coffin of the person who had died. Explain that this 'Book of the Dead' belonged to a very wealthy, important scribe called Ani who lived in Thebes around 1275 BC.

Now give them copies of the image to look at carefully in their pairs. Encourage them to annotate the image (you could use the layers of inference grid here to help guide their work).

Ask them to think about the following questions:

- Where is Ani in the image? Why do you think this?
- Who might the person wearing the mask of Anubis be?
- What are the women in the image doing and why?
- What belongings can you spot? Where do you think these are being taken?

Bring the pupils back together and encourage them to share their ideas. Explain that Ani is to the right of the procession, already in his coffin. A priest dressed as Anubis (the jackal-headed god of embalming) stands behind him, whilst another priest (the lector-priest) stands reading prayers from a scroll. The family are walking behind the coffin; Ani's son is wearing a panther skin and his wife Tutu kneels at her husband's feet. Professional female mourners (people who have been paid to cry) are gathered together, and many of Ani's servants are also there, carrying the belongings he will need for the afterlife.

At the funeral, a series of rituals would have been performed by the priests. This was all done to make sure that the dead person had everything they needed to survive in the afterlife.

⭐ Main activity

Explain that pupils will look at two further documents relating to rituals performed at the funeral. Working in pairs, pupils look at each image in turn and answer the questions below.

Weighing of the heart of Ani

Questions:

- What can you see in the image?
- What do you think might be happening?
- How might this ritual help Ani enter the afterlife?

Description:

This image shows Ani's judgement in the Hall of Judgement or Hall of Two Truths. The Egyptians believed that your heart had to be weighed and needed to be lighter than a feather in order to enter the afterlife. This image shows the scales in the centre and the god Anubis to the right. Thoth, the scribe of the gods, is behind Anubis, ready to write down Ani's judgement. Behind Thoth is a monster who will eat Ani's heart if he does not pass this test. The top of the image shows the great gods of Egypt who will pass judgement on Ani.

Equipment for opening of the mouth ceremony

Questions:

- What can you see in the photograph?
- What do you think these objects were made from?
- What do you think they were used for?

Description:

These are different utensils that were used for the most important ritual, the opening of the mouth ceremony. In this ritual, it was believed that the dead person would be able to eat, drink and move around in the afterlife. Cups and vases were used for sacred liquids during the ritual, and a special instrument was used for touching the mouth of the mummy.

Gather the pupils back together. What have they found interesting in the different documents? Why? Explain that these are just a few examples of some of the rituals that had to be performed before the dead person could enter the afterlife. Those who passed the final weighing of the heart could live for eternity in the fields of reeds.

✏️ Creative activity

Pupils could research and illustrate the different stages of the journey through the afterlife.

Copyright © Clare Horrie and Rachel Hillman, 2020

Worksheet: Layers of inference

Questions

Inferences

Observations

Document image

Life in Ancient Egypt

⊙ Lesson overview

Lesson enquiry question

What can an Egyptian tomb reveal about life in Ancient Egypt?

Resources required

Sources:

1. Photograph of the Pyramids, Giza, Egypt.
2. Nebamun hunting in the marshes.
3. A feast for Nebamun.
4. Nebamun's garden.

Lesson focus

Describe:

Describe some of the different images used in Nebamun's tomb.

Explain:

Explain some features of Ancient Egyptian life, using the tomb images.

Curriculum link:

An overview of where and when the first civilisations appeared, and a depth study of one of the following: Ancient Sumer, The Indus Valley, Ancient Egypt, The Shang Dynasty of Ancient China.

1 Photograph of the Pyramids, Giza, Egypt.

2 Nebamun hunting in the marshes. © Photo 12/ Universal Images Group via Getty Images.

3 A feast for Nebamun. © Werner Forman/Universal Images Group/Getty Images.

4 Nebamun's garden. © Universal History Archive/ Universal Images Group via Getty Images.

Copyright © Clare Horrie and Rachel Hillman, 2020

🚀 Starter activity

Display the image of the Pyramids at Giza on the whiteboard. Ask the pupils to take a few minutes looking at the photograph and then feed back on the things that they can see. Now ask the pupils:

- What type of document is this?
- Where do you think the photograph was taken?
- What do you think these structures (pyramids) were used for?

Explain to the pupils that this is a photograph of the Pyramids at Giza in Egypt. Although this photograph was taken in the 1920s, the Pyramids actually date back thousands of years (3,000 years before the birth of Christ). The Ancient Egyptians are remembered for many reasons, and the Pyramids that they left behind still stand today. They were used as giant tombs for the dead pharaohs (kings) and were built by thousands of people without the help of modern machines. After death, the pharaohs and wealthy Egyptians would have their bodies mummified and buried in their tombs with everything that they might need for the afterlife. This included jewellery, weapons and even chariots! The walls of the tombs were painted with beautiful pictures, often showing images of the deceased person enjoying the afterlife.

✏️ Creative activity

Pupils could design their own tomb images for a personality today, perhaps a favourite film star or singer. What images would they choose to illustrate and why? If a historian were to find these images in the future, what would they reveal about life today?

⭐ Main activity

Explain that in this lesson the pupils are going to look at some images that were taken from the tomb of an Ancient Egyptian called Nebamun. Nebamun was not a pharaoh, but he was a rich and important scribe in Thebes. The images in his tomb can tell us about Nebamun and they also reveal information about life in Ancient Egypt.

Ask the pupils to work in pairs, and spend time looking at the remaining three images in turn and answering the questions below for each. You could work through the first image as a whole class and model the process.

- What can you see in the image?
- What do you think the image tells us about Nebamun?
- What does the image reveal about life in Ancient Egypt?

Gather the pupils together and ask them to feed back their findings on each image. You can offer them the full description for each image as below.

Nebamun hunting in the marshes

This image shows Nebamun hunting in the marshes with his wife Hatshepsut, his daughter and their cat. It reveals information about Egyptian dress, how they hunted for animals that lived along the river banks, and how scribes wrote using hieroglyphs. The hieroglyphs on this image say that 'Nebamun is enjoying himself looking at good things.'

A feast for Nebamun

This image shows a lavish feast in honour of Nebamun. Serving girls wait on his guests, and the guests are richly dressed and have lots of delicious food to eat. Rich Egyptians would eat food such as meats, figs, cakes and dates, whereas poorer Egyptians would eat simple food such as bread, vegetables and fruit.

Nebamun's garden

This shows Nebamun's garden in the afterlife. There is a pool of fish and birds, as well as flowers and trees to provide shade. There are also fruit trees (dates). There is a goddess to the right of the pool offering Nebamun fruit and drinks. This garden is like the gardens of wealthy Egyptians, who would have had beautiful gardens outside their homes. The fish in the pools were often used for food as well as being ornamental.

Once you've looked at each image as a class, ask the pupils what they have found surprising or interesting in the images from Nebamun's tomb and why. Explain that these are just a few of the many images from Nebamun's tomb, and that they are all on display at the British Museum.

Ancient Greece

⟳ Lesson overview

Lesson enquiry question

What can artefacts reveal about life in Ancient Greece?

Resources required

Sources:

❶ Greek theatre mask.

❷ Bronze helmet of Corinthian type.

❸ Bronze cuirass (breastplate).

❹ Black-figured drinking cup showing ploughing and sowing.

❺ Black-figured storage jar showing olive gathering.

❻ Image of Ancient Greek medical practice (this is optional and various possible images for this source can easily be found by searching 'Ancient Greek medicine' on the internet).

Lesson focus

Describe:

Describe some features of life and achievements in Ancient Greece.

Explain:

Explain some of the ways in which Ancient Greek life has had an influence on the Western world.

Curriculum link:

Ancient Greece – a study of Greek life and achievements and their influence on the Western world.

❶ Greek theatre mask. © The Trustees of the British Museum.

❷ Bronze helmet of Corinthian type. © Leemage/Corbis via Getty Images.

Copyright © Clare Horrie and Rachel Hillman, 2020

🚀 Starter activity

Ask the pupils to work in pairs with one person as A and the other as B. Ask all As to look at the whiteboard and all Bs to close their eyes. Display the image of the Greek theatre mask (source 1) on the whiteboard. Ask the As to take one minute looking at the image before you remove it from the whiteboard. Now ask them to describe what they have seen to their partners (the Bs). All the Bs should then draw what has been described to them.

Now show the image again on the whiteboard and ask all of the pupils to take a careful look. Ask the Bs how accurate their partner's description of the image was. Ask the As what they remembered to tell their partner and what they didn't notice and tell their partners about. Explain to the pupils that this activity was all about studying an image very carefully and making observations.

Ask the pairs to now talk to each other about what they can see in the image. You can use the following prompts if needed:

- What can you see in the image? (Encourage the pupils to describe everything that they can see in the features of the face.)
- What do you think this object was used for? Why do you think this? (Encourage the pupils to link their inferences back to their initial observations.)
- When do you think this object was used or made? Why do you think this?

Once the pupils have had an opportunity to feed back their observations, explain to them that they are looking at an image of an Ancient Greek theatre mask. The masks worn by actors at this time in performances would have been made from stiffened and painted linen, which means that none of them have survived. This mask is a model made from terracotta; because theatre was so popular in Ancient Greece, models of masks and actors were made out of stone to decorate buildings. Images were also used in mosaics and paintings. Explain that this mask was worn by an old-man character in comedies of the 300s BC; draw the pupils' attention to the large smile, wrinkled forehead and lack of hair. He is wearing a wreath of leaves and berries on his head.

Explain to the pupils that Greek theatre was a very important feature of life in Ancient Greece. Plays were performed at festivals and thousands of people would attend to watch. There would have been music and colourful costumes to set the scene, and the plays were often about right and wrong, and the powers of the gods. Ask the pupils why they think the actors would wear masks during a performance. Talk about the idea of masks and disguise, and how they could transform the actors into many different characters. Masks were central to the theatre of the performance.

Talk about how theatre in Ancient Greece has had an impact and influenced theatre in the Western world today. You could touch on, for example, the fact that themes such as superheroes and monsters are timeless. They were used in Ancient Greek stories but are still present in many plays and stories today.

❸ Bronze cuirass (breastplate). © Leemage/ Universal Images Group via Getty Images.

❹ Black-figured drinking cup showing ploughing and sowing. © The Trustees of the British Museum.

❺ Black-figured storage jar showing olive gathering. © The Trustees of the British Museum.

⭐ Main activity

Explain to the pupils that they are going to look at some further images of artefacts to see what else they can find out about life in Ancient Greece. Ask the pupils to work in their pairs, and spend time looking at each image in turn and answering the questions below. Afterwards, gather the pupils together and ask them to feed back their findings. Once they have offered their own observations and interpretations, you can provide the full description of each image and how Ancient Greece has influenced Western civilisation as below.

Images 1 and 2: Ancient Greek armour (bronze helmet and breastplate)

Questions:

- What can you see in the images? What do you think these items are?
- Who might have worn them?
- What do they reveal about life in Ancient Greece?
- What does this tell us about the impact of Ancient Greek civilisation on the Western world today?

Description:

These images show two different sections of Greek armour. The first image shows a bronze helmet and the second image shows a breastplate that would have been joined at the shoulders and sides, by straps and buckles. Both are designed to protect a Greek soldier in combat. The Greek city states were frequently at war with each other. By the fifth century BC, soldiers had become well armed and highly trained. The rich fought as hoplites (they held a hopla, a large, round shield). The less well-off served as peltasts, and were more lightly armed than their hoplite comrades.

Impact on Western civilisation:

The Ancient Greeks' military techniques were used and replicated by other civilisations, including the Romans. Their use of armour to protect soldiers, teamwork to make defensive formations and speeches to rouse the soldiers before battle are all good examples of this.

Images 3 and 4: Black-figured drinking cup showing ploughing and sowing and black-figured storage jar showing olive gathering

Questions:

- What can you see in the images?
- What do you think the people are doing?
- What do they reveal about life in Ancient Greece?
- What does this tell us about the impact of Ancient Greek civilisation on the Western world today?

Description:

These images are taken from a drinking cup and storage jar, and show different types of farming taking place. The cup shows ploughing and sowing of crops (preparing the land and then sowing the seed), whilst the jar shows olive gathering. A small boy sits in a tree shaking down the olives, whilst two other men beat the tree with sticks to encourage more olives to fall. A fourth figure gathers the fallen olives in a basket at the foot of the tree. The Ancient Greeks grew many different crops, including wheat, barley and vegetables. Fruit trees were grown so that people could eat olives, pears, apples and figs. Most people grew their own crops to feed their families, and any spare was sold at market.

Impact on Western civilisation:

Greek food and influences were spread via Ancient Rome throughout Europe, including the use of grapes for wine.

Image 5: Ancient Greek medicine (optional)

You could find an image (using the internet) that could be used to investigate Ancient Greek medicine to provide another area of enquiry. The Ancient Greeks studied medicine and disease in a scientific way. They studied symptoms and tried to provide practical treatments and cures. The most famous Greek doctor was Hippocrates and many medical pupils still take the Hippocratic Oath today.

Once you have worked through the images as a class, ask the pupils what they have found surprising or interesting in the different documents about the Ancient Greeks. Have they seen any similarities between life in Ancient Greece and life today?

Explain that these are just a few examples of some of the different ways in which Ancient Greek civilisation influenced the Western world. As a research or homework task, ask the pupils to choose an area of enquiry to find out more about what other achievements in Ancient Greece have influenced life today. There are lots of examples, such as language, mathematics, ideas of democracy and government, inventions, and so on.

✏️ Creative activity

Pupils could design and make their own Greek theatre masks. You could even write a class play for the pupils to perform in their masks!

Copyright © Clare Horrie and Rachel Hillman, 2020

Benin power of the Oba

⊙ Lesson overview

Lesson enquiry question

What do the 'Benin Bronzes' show us about the power of the Oba?

Resources required

Sources:

1 Oba and attendants.

2 Oba holding leopards.

Lesson focus

Describe:

Describe the 'Benin Bronzes' and what they depict.

Explain:

Explain that the Kingdom of Benin (modern south-west Nigeria) was an important power in West Africa until the end of the 19th century when the British took the Kingdom under their control by force.

Curriculum link:

A non-European society that provides contrasts with British history – the Kingdom of Benin.

1 Oba and attendants. © The Trustees of the British Museum.

2 Oba holding leopards. © The Trustees of the British Museum.

Copyright © Clare Horrie and Rachel Hillman, 2020

🚀 Starter activity

Reveal source 1 as a mystery document to get pupils thinking. After accepting some initial observations, you can explain that this plaque shows an Oba (a ruler) surrounded by his attendants, two of whom are holding up their shields in a protective manner. This has been identified as Oba Esigie, one of the rulers of the Kingdom of Benin. Benin was a kingdom located in modern south-west Nigeria. It was an important power in West Africa until the end of the 19th century, when the British took the Kingdom under their control by force.

As a coastal kingdom, the people of Benin traded with Europeans and were able to dominate trade inland. The Portuguese first started to trade with Benin in 1489. Over 400 years later, in the reign of Queen Victoria, the British were keen to expand their Empire and wanted to bring the Kingdom under their control. They did this by force, captured the Oba, destroyed his palace and removed many art works, including this source.

Returning to source 1, discuss the following:

- How can we recognise the Oba (king)? (Look for the wide-beaded choker; a multi-row necklace of agate and rare coral beads – believed to have spiritual powers; large agate pendants hanging on the sides of the coral-beaded cap, with feathers; arm and foot rings; and a decorated fabric cloth with belt and hip decoration.)
- Why do you think the Oba was dressed in this way?
- What does the Oba hold in his left hand? (It is a ceremonial switch – a thin stick usually used for beating animals.)
- What are the naked attendants carrying? (They have a ceremonial sword and a box to present gifts.)
- Can you explain what the taller attendants are doing? Why? (They are protecting the Oba's head, shading him from the sun, which suggests he is important.)
- Why are the smallest attendants naked? (It shows they are less important.)
- Can you describe the hairstyles of all the attendants? What does this suggest about the scene? (It is a stylised ritual and a special occasion.)
- What does the background of the plaque look like?
- What might the holes in the plaque be used for?

You can now explain that this is one of the brass plaques that was used to decorate the wooden pillars, beams and gates of the royal palace in Benin City, and dates from 1550 to 1650. The plaques show details of the Oba or king. Some plaques show historical events, commemorate successful wars or reveal aspects of court life or ritual. They are called the 'Benin Bronzes' but are made of leaded brass. The depicted scene on this plaque probably represents a ritual at a palace ceremony, the Igue. The Igue was the king's festival that lasted nine days and was celebrated at the end of the year. The Oba's powers were renewed and the people and land blessed.

⭐ Main activity

Pupils will now look at another of the 'Benin Bronzes'. Show them source 2 on printouts or a whiteboard, and give them dimensions to work out the real-life size:

Height: 49 centimetres

Width: 34 centimetres

Depth: 6 centimetres

Then pupils discuss the following questions in pairs:

- Who does this figure represent?
- Describe his clothing. (It's fringed with bells.)
- What does he wear on his wrists? (Broad bronze or ivory armlets.)
- What does he wear on his legs? (Coral beads.)
- What creature forms his belt? (A mudfish. The mudfish is able to leave the water and live on land. Oba are sometimes shown with mudfish legs to show that the Oba live in the land of men and the world of the gods.)
- What is the Oba holding? (Leopards wearing collars with small hawk-bells, suggesting they are tame.)
- What does this plaque suggest about the power of the Oba? (He has control over the leopard, king of the forest, which suggests the Oba's power).
- How is the plaque decorated? (It has raised rosettes to represent flowers.)

After working through the questions, pupils can try to write a caption for this plaque, before thinking about the following:

- What does neither plaque show us? (Women, children, ordinary village life, poverty, crops and townspeople.)
- What can we learn about trade from these plaques? (They must have traded to get the brass to make it. Coral shows that Benin traded with the Mediterranean.)

✏️ Creative activity

In groups, pupils research one of the following Benin festivals and ceremonies: the Igue (Oba); the Ague (first yams blessed in hope of plentiful harvest); Ugie Ivie (Festival of Beads – the Oba's coral regalia dipped in cow's blood to give it spiritual power); Ugie Erha Oba (honouring the Oba's paternal ancestors); or Oduduwa (celebrating the Oba's ancestors). They should collate materials and write short explanations for their festival or ceremony, which you can use to create a class display.

Copyright © Clare Horrie and Rachel Hillman, 2020

Benin trade

⟳ Lesson overview

Lesson enquiry question

What can objects tell us about trade in the Kingdom of Benin?

Resources required

Sources:

❶ Portuguese soldier figure made of bronze.

❷ Carved ivory mask, inlaid with iron and bronze.

Lesson focus

Describe:

Describe how these two objects offer opportunities to explore Benin's trade with the Portuguese.

Explain:

Explain that the Kingdom of Benin was an important power in West Africa until the end of the 19th century. As a coastal kingdom, the people of Benin traded with Europeans and were able to dominate trade inland. The Portuguese first started to trade with Benin in 1489.

Curriculum link:

A non-European society that provides contrasts with British history – the Kingdom of Benin.

❶ Portuguese soldier figure made of bronze.
© The Trustees of the British Museum.

❷ Carved ivory mask, inlaid with iron and bronze.
© Werner Forman/Universal Images Group/
Getty Images.

🚀 Starter activity

Reveal source 1 as a mystery object to get pupils thinking. You can either print it out or project it on a whiteboard. Show the pupils the actual size of the object; its height is 37.5 centimetres. What can the pupils see? What do they think this object might be?

You can now explain that this is a piece of art from the Kingdom of Benin. If necessary, remind the pupils that Benin was a kingdom located in modern south-west Nigeria. It was an important power in West Africa until the end of the 19th century when the British took the Kingdom under their control by force and took art works, including this source and another you will look at later in the lesson.

Tell the pupils that the source is a Portuguese soldier figure made of bronze. Figures like this were kept on royal altars or on the roof of the royal palace and often appear in Benin art. Pupils now discuss in pairs what they observe:

- What four items suggest he is a soldier? (Guide them towards the helmet, gun, sword and armour.)
- Can you describe his face?
- Can you suggest why the king of Benin sometimes used Portuguese soldiers in the Kingdom of Benin?

Explain that the Portuguese traded brass bracelets with the Oba in return for pepper, ivory, leopard skins and people taken as slaves to work in Portuguese colonies in Brazil. It is from this brass that craftsmen created the famous Bronzes of Benin City. Portuguese traders often appear in Benin art. They are shown with long hair and noses, and weapons. As these Europeans reached Benin by sea, they were often linked to the god Olokun, ruler of the sea and provider of wealth. It was said that the Oba defeated this god and took his wealth, so the display of European figures might celebrate this. The Portuguese long continued to appear in Benin art after they had ceased contact with Benin.

⭐ Main activity

Tell the pupils that you are going to look at another object from the Kingdom of Benin. Print out copies of source 2 or project it on a whiteboard. Show them the actual size of the object:

Height: 24.5 centimetres

Width: 12.5 centimetres

Depth: 6 centimetres

Ask the pupils whether they think this mask is male or female. Can they explain why? You can then explain to the pupils that the mask was supposed to represent Idia, mother of Oba Esigie, and was worn by the Oba on the hip during important ceremonies. It is a rare image of a woman. Also the mask was made of ivory, a material that attracted the Portuguese to trade with Benin.

Now discuss the following questions to explore what the pupils can see and evaluate:

- What can you see at the top of the mask? (There are heads representing the Portuguese.)
- Why do you think the Portuguese appear on the mask? (They symbolise Benin's alliance with and control over Europeans.)
- Can you describe the collar?
- How would you describe the expression of the face?
- What does this mask suggest about the Oba? (They relied on ceremony and symbolism to show their power.)

🖋 Creative activity

As a class, find more images of the art of Benin, including the 'Bronzes' in the British Museum collections online. The pupils can role play an interview with the curator of the museum, discussing their importance as historical sources and whether the 'Bronzes' should return to museums in Nigeria.

Copyright © Clare Horrie and Rachel Hillman, 2020